D0500028

THE LAST DAY
OF MY LIFE

Jim Moret

Library of Congress Cataloging-in-Publication Data
Moret, Jim.
    The last day of my life / Jim Moret.
        p. cm.
    ISBN 978-0-9827876-0-1 (hardcover)
1. Moret, Jim. 2. Television journalists--United States--Biography. I. Title.
    PN4874.M584A3 2009
    070.92--dc22
    [B]

                                                    2010908738

Book Design by The Imagists

Printed in the United States of America

10 9 8 7 6 5 4 3 2

DEDICATION

For my beloved "MACK."
Matthew, Amanda, Carly and Keri.
You saved my life.

TABLE OF CONTENTS

THE CHALLENGE

FOR MOST OF MY ADULT LIFE, I HAVE TOLD OTHER PEOPLE'S STORIES. It was my job, my passion and my purpose.

I have spent more than twenty-five years interviewing people on television—first as a reporter for KABC-TV in Los Angeles and then as a reporter/anchor for KCBS. Next, I co-hosted a national entertainment show for Fox and then co-anchored various news programs on CNN. I am currently Chief Correspondent for the nationally syndicated television news magazine, *Inside Edition.* During the course of my career, I regularly sat down with celebrities, politicians, criminal defendants, and victims of crimes, accidents, and natural disasters. They were ordinary people in extraordinary situations: people who cheated death in tornadoes and floods, and others who faced enormous challenges, like those with terminal illness. Some of those individuals who later succumbed to their disease did so with quiet resolve and dignity.

Some of the stories I covered were heartbreaking. I spoke to a woman in Texas whose husband had run off with their three children and their family's life savings, leaving her to struggle alone. I met a family who narrowly escaped death when their Southern California home was buried under twenty feet of mud and debris. The hillside above them gave way following a torrential downpour. I sat alongside a badly injured and shaken woman who lay in a hospital bed in Utah after her husband intentionally flipped the small plane they were flying onto its side when he saw they were about to crash. He knew he was sacrificing his own life in order to save hers.

As a journalist, I always strive to tell their stories fairly, accurately and completely. Above all, I try to tell them with respect.

Then, suddenly, after more than two decades of asking questions of *others*, I was confronted with the toughest assignment of all: asking questions of *myself*. Now, the camera was turned on me, and I had to answer the single most important question of all—**do I want to live**?

Before I could decide whether I wanted to move forward, I first had to look back and understand the stories of my life, just as I had examined the stories of so many others' lives over the past two and half decades in front of the camera.

I issued myself an unusual challenge: to imagine that I had been told, in no uncertain terms, that I had only twenty-four hours left to live. What would I do if I knew that this was the last day of my life? There were no other conditions attached. I felt fine—perfectly healthy, but with one major caveat, namely, a definite expiration date. Whom would I want to see? Where would I choose to spend my final hours? Would I make apologies or offer forgiveness? Would I use it as a time to seek out one last great adventure? These were some of the questions that I began to ask myself, over and over again.

It became an obsession.

I recognized immediately the built-in limitations of this bizarre hypothetical question. I was essentially challenging myself to search out those people and things that were most important to me and which make me happy in the present. In this scenario, by definition, delayed gratification is denied gratification.

While the premise may, at first blush, appear negative, the real purpose and the final impact was quite the opposite. I see now how that single provocative question, *"What would I do on the last day of my life?"* led me on a journey of self-examination and exploration. It was a painful and arduous path. Without realizing it, I began an odyssey toward self-empowerment, challenging myself to *choose* how I want to live the *rest* of my life—whether it was for twenty-four more *hours* or twenty-four more *years.*

That somber query actually became a surprisingly liberating exercise. I was stripped to the barest and most basic of inquests, the most vital question there is: *what is really important in life?*

WHAT WENT WRONG?

BY MOST ACCOUNTS, I SEEMED TO HAVE IT ALL. I have what many people would consider a glamorous job on television, regularly interviewing celebrities and traveling the country to cover major national news stories. I have been blessed with a long marriage to a loving and beautiful wife who after more than twenty-five years, still makes me smile. Together, we are raising three unique, talented kids. We live in a cozy Spanish-style home in a charming neighborhood almost walking distance from the famed Beverly Hilton Hotel, where the Golden Globes are held every year. From the outside looking in, my life appeared to be almost idyllic, and from my early adulthood, I seemed destined to have everything I could ever want.

I began my television career in Los Angeles. Following a brief stint practicing law in California, and armed with little more than a degree in Communication Studies from UCLA and tons of moxie, I approached the general manager at the ABC-owned station where my wife worked selling ad time and persuaded him to put me on the air as a legal reporter. This was back in 1983—a blissful time when there were no twenty-four hour cable channels with talking heads, no self-proclaimed experts espousing theories on high-profile court cases, and virtually no "TV lawyers." That first job, appearing once a week on an afternoon talk show, launched my broadcast career. I eventually persuaded the news director to hire me as a General Assignment reporter.

Within a few years, I was anchoring the morning newscast on the rival CBS Los Angeles station. Three years after that, I was hired to co-host a nationally syndicated entertainment news program for Fox. It was short-lived, lasting only one season, but it was my first national job, and it led to bigger and better assignments.

For the second decade of my career, I enjoyed a near meteoric rise at CNN. I began as Senior Entertainment Correspondent, and within a year I was anchoring the network's daily entertainment program, *Showbiz Today*. I was then thrust into the national spotlight as Chief Anchor for the network's gavel-to-gavel coverage of the O.J. Simpson murder trial. I was simply at the right place at the right time. I had now parlayed my background as a lawyer and a journalist into a unique hybrid position, straddling both news and entertainment. When I left the network in 2001, I was co-anchoring *Showbiz Today* and CNN's main newscast of record, *The World Today*, along with Wolf Blitzer and Joie Chen. I was earning close to three quarters of a million dollars a year.

I earned a great living. I had a beautiful wife, Keri, and three fantastic kids. *What could I know about grief and anguish?* How could I possibly have any complaints that would lead me to contemplate the last day of my life?

You'd be surprised.

Every job I had in broadcasting was followed by another position that offered more responsibility and more money than the job before it. I had, understandably, been lulled into believing that pattern would continue unabated. Whether it was misplaced pride or arrogance, I believed that after leaving CNN and taking a couple of months off, I would soon be anchoring a new show on another network earning my previous salary or even more. *My hubris was my downfall.*

Occasional hosting jobs came my way. Some of them were fairly lucrative. Still, the meaningful next step in my career was replaced by a series of professional missteps. It took more than two and a half years to land another full-time job. That long delay proved agonizing and humiliating. It was a blow to my ego, to be sure, but it was also a personal financial disaster.

Though my income had stopped, the mortgage and other bills continued unabated. I had grown up in Los Angeles, and Keri was raised in Beverly Hills. We felt then, and continue to believe, that the gift of a fine education is the most worthwhile sacrifice a parent can make for their child. All three of our children attended private school beginning with kindergarten. The benefits are apparent when talking with any of our kids. They are well rounded, confident and enriched because of the experience, but the financial costs have been staggering. *Each month we fell deeper in debt.*

Even on reflection, it seemed inconceivable that I could have dug such a deep hole for my family. I had an escape clause—or so I thought. The real estate market was booming, and our million-dollar home was now valued at nearly two and a half million dollars. That inflation provided me a seemingly endless financial safety net in a single word: refinancing. I found myself dipping into that reservoir of funds again and again in an effort to stay afloat, to remain current on our mortgage.

It ended up being a temporary fix and, in fact, only compounded the problem.

My growing desperation prompted me to commit the single biggest financial error of my life. Like millions of Americans, I fell under the spell of instant gratification offered by a sub-prime home loan. The lure of a manageable house payment, guaranteed for a few years, would surely give me enough time to regain my professional footing. That's what I thought, anyway. Reading about tens of thousands of people across the country losing their homes to foreclosure, some of them well-known celebrities, proved no consolation whatsoever. Whether your home is worth $150,000 or $5 million, the real prospect of losing everything you have worked your entire life to achieve is devastating and utterly demoralizing.

Eventually, the grace period on our sub-prime loan drew to a close, and our payments were set to escalate to nearly $10,000 a month. Making matters even worse, selling the house was no longer a viable option. Because of the market's precipitous fall, our home was now worth *less* than the amount we owed on it. As a result, I not only faced losing my home, but also defaulting on our mortgage and wiping out my good credit for years to come.

I had either failed or simply refused to see that I was trapped in an endless and dangerous cycle prompted by the lure of easy refinancing. I was in trouble from the moment

I signed my name to that last loan document, only I didn't know it at the time. Sometimes, even as adults, we fall back into that childhood trap of believing that tomorrow will never come. But bills always become due. It is inevitable. Perhaps as we grow older we also become more adept at kidding ourselves.

The timing of this impending crisis only heightened my sense of despair and hopelessness. My financial meltdown did not hit when I was out of work, but rather several years *after* my career was already back on track. I had reestablished my career, and it was even on an upward swing. I was Chief Correspondent on the nationally syndicated television news magazine *Inside Edition*. I was also a regular guest and analyst on CNN and FOX and frequently appeared on MSNBC.

That was the tragic irony of my situation. Outwardly, everything appeared fine. It wasn't fine at all. Not by a long shot. The fuse was lit on this financial time bomb, and it was apparent to me that nothing could prevent it from going off. I believed there was no simple way out.

Desperation weakens the spirit and damages the soul. It prompted some of the most self-destructive thoughts I could imagine. Before long, I could not even keep those thoughts to myself. I began to joke about being more valuable to my family *dead* than *alive*. After all, I had a $3 million life insurance policy. What I said in jest led me down a dark and dangerous path. I would regularly lay awake, night after night, worrying and then wondering in all seriousness:

"AM I BETTER OFF DEAD?"

It wasn't simply for a night or two that these morbid thoughts would haunt me. It became a terrifying ritual. How many times would I wake in a start with my wife slumbering peacefully beside me? Our children fast asleep, oblivious to the overwhelming anguish that I was enduring in the next room. My heart began to race uncontrollably. Often I wondered whether I was, in fact, about to suffer a heart attack. My mind began to play out the scene of my own funeral in excruciating detail. I saw the casket, my casket, closed and positioned at the front of the congregation. The sound of weeping was unmistakable. I saw people I had not seen for years alongside my family and friends, their eyes puffy and red, filling the chapel to capacity and beyond, spilling into the courtyard. So many mourners, gathered to pay their final respects. What would they say about me? How would they remember me? I could hear my family and friends weeping. The people who had been closest to me in life were now clearly saddened by my passing. It almost seemed real.

Eventually, I grew to dread the night. I would often seek the emotional solace that only the sofa and television would offer, but it proved to be just a brief respite from my despair. The hours until daylight often seemed endless. I needed rest, but none came. I would find myself at the kitchen table having coffee, hours before my day should have begun. Soon, the cycle would start all over again. I began to fear there was no escape except for the ultimate refuge that only death could bring. The topic had consumed my thoughts for months. Each night, the mental exercise would begin where the previous night had ended. It was a seamless, macabre mental movie.

The inevitable questions would follow: Is there life after death? What is the meaning of life in the first place?

I recall mentioning my constant fixation with dying to some friends one night while at a dinner party. The conversation came to an abrupt halt as everyone at the table turned to see if I was joking, as I am known to do regularly. But they soon realized that this was not a joke. *"What do you mean you think of death?" they asked. "I think about dying every night," I said, as a matter of fact.* They were stunned to see that I was serious. Their silence revealed their discomfort and concern, and I quickly dropped it.

Ultimately, my constant and regular focus on death turned from the *what if* to the *how.* Dark thoughts are like a cancer, and if unchecked and unchallenged, they can overtake you. At least mine did. Eventually, this morbid obsession intruded upon my waking moments.

I finally frightened myself when I actually saw my own suicide play out in my mind.

I remember the moment with utter, chilling clarity. I was driving to an interview through a mountainous and particularly dangerous canyon north of Los Angeles. It was a narrow, winding road, and hairpin turns rendered speeds of even twenty-five miles an hour unsafe. I was amazed how close I was to the busy Pacific Coast Highway and yet how far away it felt from civilization. It was so quiet here, so remote, overlooking an undeveloped canyon just a few miles off the main roadway into Malibu. In the distance, I could see the ocean, calm and peaceful. I felt completely alone. Even though I have lived in this city my entire life, I had never seen this particular stretch of road before. I was struck by the treacherous nature of the drive and the surprising absence of guardrails along the cliff's edge. Just two feet to the right of my tires, the pavement gave way to loose gravel, and, just beyond that, the hillside was particularly steep. The drop was at least a hundred feet. The terrain, while covered with trees and thick brush, was also littered with heavy rocks and boulders. I knew it was dangerous enough to prove fatal should I turn too sharply, too quickly. The sky was clear, and the bright sunlight reflected off my windshield, forcing me to remain in a lower gear to keep my speed down. As my car's engine raced, so did my mind, focusing on the darkest of thoughts. I imagined how easy it would be to intentionally miss a turn and plummet to almost certain death into the canyon below. I was confident that it would be difficult to even spot my car at the bottom of the ravine. By the time someone discovered me, it would be too late. I was convinced that it would look like an accident, so my family would at least benefit from my life-insurance coverage.

They were the most dangerous five words I have ever uttered: I wish I were dead. It prompted my somber recognition that this could be more than an impulsive declaration of frustration and could instead signal one final, fatal act.

Would I really have gone through with it? I say "No," primarily because I didn't. Still, the vividness and detail of this perverse mental exercise truly frightened me. That is when I fully realized the magnitude and depth of my depression. Something had to be done, and soon.

It was in this blackest moment that I had an epiphany.

It was similar to the famous scene in the Frank Capra classic *It's a Wonderful Life,* where Jimmy Stewart is about to jump off a bridge, and an angel-in-training asks him if he would like to see what the world would be like if he had never lived. Like Stewart's character, intense financial stress and pressures had literally blinded me to the simplest and most important joys in my own life. But my question to myself didn't center on what if I had *never lived,* but rather what if I had *one day left to live.* How would I react? What would I choose to cherish and appreciate? What was really important after all? I am a reporter. Why not take on the story of my life to search out the answers?

It was a provocative question and a dramatic turning point in my journey from darkness into the light. *That moment of imagining my own suicide in detail actually began my journey toward rediscovering the beauty, value and love that already existed around me.* I recalled a light caress and gentle kiss from my wife, the unprovoked "I love you, Dad," from my eleven-year- old son and watching my mother fight for each day, following a devastating disease and liver transplant. These all reminded me of the profound value of each moment we are given in this life. It was a gift that I was both squandering and ignoring. But I needed to dig much deeper than that.

The same single question continued to haunt me.

What if I knew that this was my last day? How would I choose to spend it? Could I use this as a template for how best to truly live rather than simply survive? Would it convince me to choose life over death?

First, I needed to honestly examine what is truly important and meaningful in my life. That meant taking a hard and, at times, a sobering look back at the relationships and events that shaped me throughout my life. My life was a collage of moments and experiences. It was defined by acts of friendship and love, gratitude and understanding, apology and forgiveness, music and laughter, hope and redemption.

This is an account of my personal journey of self-discovery, successfully passing through the darkness to reach my eventual salvation. As a journalist, I have attempted to approach every story with honesty. But this was not just *any* story. This was *my* story.

FRIENDSHIP

As a child, my parents used to tell me that if I were lucky, I would be able to count my true friends on one hand. I felt fortunate to have two such friends fairly early in life. To this day, I resist calling anyone my *best* friend because the two people I once called that were both taken from me far too soon. Their time here may have been brief, but their imprint on my life was not. Even the title "best friend" is inadequate when describing my relationships with Steve and Josh. They mark in a serial fashion my journey from childhood into adulthood. Losing them both, one after the other, still leaves a profound emptiness in my life all these years later. I honor their memory and cherish our time together.

"Friendship makes prosperity
more shining and lessens adversity
by dividing and sharing it."
—Cicero (106 BC-43 BC)

STEVE

I met Steve when I was nine years old. My family had just moved to a new neighborhood in the hills above Los Angeles. Steve was the first person I met. He lived down the street in our new development of tract homes. We soon became fast friends. Steve was bold where I was timid. He was spontaneous where I was often reserved. If opposites attract, it's easy to understand the glue that bound us together, almost from the start. We had similar likes but completely different approaches to life.

Our first two summers together were spent playing in the new homes still under construction. We built our very first fort together in the brush on the hillside above our houses. Every day was a wild adventure, even if it only meant riding bikes or playing ball. We were inseparable, and together we were invincible. Or so we thought.

Less than two years later, Steve, still in the sixth grade, began to complain of terrible headaches. He missed day after day of school. At first, I thought he was faking in order to get out of class. It was my first lesson that being a child offers no protection from the harsh realities of the world. I remember feeling horribly guilty when I discovered that the source of Steve's headaches was serious: he had a malignant brain tumor. His parents were told that the tumor was operable, and hopes were high that Steve could not only be saved, but cured. To a kid, that belief in Steve's full recovery was almost mandatory. Imagining anything less was impossible.

Steve's surgery was a success, but his recuperation lasted for months. A hospital bed was moved into a downstairs den that now served as both his temporary bedroom and his home school. Steve wore the physical scars of his surgery for all to see. His once handsome face was now marred by a paralysis that claimed the muscles down half his body. A crooked smile and blank stare from one of his dark eyes was at first startling. But Steve's spirit proved stronger than the cancer, and nothing seemed to defeat him. I sat with him for many afternoons. We talked and played board games and watched television together. He was still my best friend, and no illness would change that. In fact, our friendship only grew stronger and more intense. Beating cancer seemed to restore and intensify his youthful sense of invulnerability. Slowly, Steve recovered, and he was finally well enough to return to school. We were just kids again.

Staring death in the face is not easy for anyone, let alone an eleven-year-old boy. Steve's lust for living life to the fullest only seemed to grow more intense. No risk was too great; nothing was too outrageous for him to try. He was never reckless, but now he was fearless.

Our friendship progressed well into our teens but that's when the tumors resurfaced, this time along Steve's spine. They eventually choked off the nerves to his legs, rendering him unable to walk. Others might have seen a teenager in a wheelchair, but to me, he was still just my friend, challenged but undaunted. I saw him cry more than once, but I still believed that he was the strongest person I had ever met.

His body was broken but, incredibly, his spirit and confidence seemed to remain unshaken. His charm overshadowed any outward appearance of disability. He had a beautiful girlfriend and was always fun to be around. I can still see his half grin and a bit of the devil in his eyes. It still makes me smile.

Steve continued to battle with the cancer that had tried so many times before to claim him. The disease finally took him when he was just nineteen, but Steve never gave into the illness. He never lost his hope or his dignity. He lived a life that was far too short and far too challenged, but he made everyone who knew him richer for it. I felt luckiest of all for having been so close to him for so long. I felt lost when he was gone.

Steve and I loved going to the movies. I vividly remember the last film we saw together. It was 1973, about a year before he died. I packed Steve's wheelchair in the trunk of my '69 Camaro and took him to see Fellini's *Amarcord*. The movie was comical and heartwarming, but for some reason I wasn't quite getting into the offbeat spirit of the movie. I was convinced that Steve didn't like it either, so we left early. After Steve passed away, his mother told me that he actually loved the film. I felt so horrible for taking that away from him. Now, I never leave a movie before it's over. I have seen *Amarcord* a few times since then, and I cry every time I watch it.

Steve's older sister had dated one of the two brothers who lived next door to me. Eventually, they married and started a family of their own. Seeing them occasionally throughout my life remains my only link to my childhood friend, whom I still miss deeply. He never grew old. He never married. But he lived. Boy, did he live. He taught me what living really meant.

"True friendship is like sound health,
the value of it is seldom known until it be lost."
—Charles Caleb Colton (1780-1832)

JOSH

Josh was my best friend throughout our college years and well beyond, into adulthood. We were always together. Josh was by my side during Steve's funeral. In fact, it was Josh who actually drove me to Steve's memorial service. I remember being too overcome with grief to drive alone. Josh was with me on some of the days that would literally define the rest of my life. He was with me when I first saw Keri, the girl who would one day become my wife. He stood as best man at our wedding and was godfather to our daughter, Carly. Josh had a lust for life that was as big as his imagination. Josh was already gone when our son, Matthew, was born. Matthew's middle name begins with the letter "J" in Josh's memory. My boy even has a dimple that often reminds me of my friend. I know they would have loved one another as dearly as I loved him.

Josh and I met in high school, and in much the same way I had experienced with Steve, there was a yin and yang duality that drew us to one another. He was an intellectual, a homebody, where I was the more extroverted class clown. Josh was one of the smartest people I have ever known, with an insatiable hunger for news, history, politics and theology. He spoke several languages, and for a time I was convinced he worked for the CIA. In fact, he told me the agency was trying to recruit him out of college. That belief was bolstered when I was tracked down and questioned about Josh at a sorority I was visiting while still in college. My interrogator, whom I will call Mr. Smith, was a rather nondescript man with horn-rimmed glasses in a black suit, white shirt and narrow black tie. Mr. Smith presented his U.S. Defense Department identification. He told me that I had been a difficult guy to locate, to which I quipped, "If you had trouble finding *me*, what are you doing in Angola?" Mr. Smith didn't laugh.

Josh had a series of unusual illnesses. In his late 20s he had mononucleosis, which put him in the hospital. We became close during his bout several years earlier with that same illness. It had forced him to miss nearly a semester of college. We spent many nights discussing world events, school and girls, while I fleeced him at gin rummy at the rate of a dime per point. I never collected on the thousands of dollars that I had "won." It didn't seem fair. But those losses proved sufficient motivation for him to eventually become quite a good player.

A few years later, Josh developed a tumor in his pituitary gland that threatened to blind him. It required a somewhat radical surgical procedure through his nostrils to remove the growth at the base of his brain. He recovered completely.

Ultimately, however, Josh met his match. In his thirties, he was diagnosed with leukemia. That battle would last several years. Those illnesses forced Josh to focus on what was important in his life—his goals, his dreams, his friends, how he wanted to live. He endured numerous chemotherapy and radiation treatments, and eventually, he underwent a painful bone marrow transplant. He fought hard because he valued every day, and he wanted as many of them as possible. For a short time, it looked like he had actually beaten the cancer that was attacking his body.

One of my fondest memories with Josh involved the simplest of pleasures. The two of us would go to The Apple Pan, a local hamburger joint in Los Angeles, built in 1941. It is famous for three things: their Hickory Burger, homemade apple pie and probably the best tuna salad sandwich in the city. It is a tiny restaurant—a small, clapboard California bungalow, the lone wooden cottage in a sea of concrete storefronts and shopping malls. The atmosphere was reminiscent of that old *Saturday Night Live* skit in the diner with John Belushi as a short order cook. Josh and I would each order a tuna on rye, a side of fries and a slice of apple pie. We would sit at the counter and discuss all sorts of things, big and small.

When things turned bleakest, and it became clear that his painful struggle was about to end, my wife and I went to Josh's bedside to say goodbye to the friend we both loved so dearly. We each took turns and sat alongside his bed and said our goodbyes as best we could. We wanted to believe that it was not really the end, but in our hearts we all knew that this was our final farewell. When Josh died, I vowed never again to call anyone my best friend.

Josh could not choose how long he would live his life—clearly, none of us can—but he did decide *how* he would live it. Josh traveled the world. He owned and ran a popular nightclub in Los Angeles. His was an odd, nocturnal lifestyle, but one that appealed to him. Still, he never stopped growing intellectually and spiritually. He was constantly reading and learning. He had a passion for both political science and philosophy. He displayed an uncanny understanding of events, both domestic and international. His father was deeply religious, and Josh shared his reverence for their faith. I always found it curious that this intellectual, almost pious man also seemed to enjoy and thrive on the somewhat seedy lifestyle of a club owner.

Ultimately, Josh also decided where he would spend his last moments. He told me that he was not afraid of dying, only that he would miss us terribly. Instead of remaining in the hospital, Josh chose to return to the house he had built and loved so much. His master bedroom was his sanctuary— unusually large but still warm and inviting, soothing and peaceful. Josh wanted to be around the things and people he cared for most, and his doctor and friend made sure this last wish was granted.

I remember the last time I held his hand and kissed my friend goodbye. I told him what he already knew—that I loved him. He was drifting in and out of consciousness from the morphine drip that was masking his pain. While I knew that part of Josh was already leaving us, his soft voice and brief smile told me that he heard my farewell. In my heart, I knew that he was soothed by his final choice. He was *where* he wanted to be. He had decided *where he wanted to spend the last day of his life.*

While I was writing this chapter, Keri came across the last birthday card I wrote to Josh. It was dated October 31, 1993. Josh died less than six weeks later. We discovered the card sitting on the nightstand in his bedroom and have kept it ever since:

Dear Josh,

Birthdays tend to serve as both a reflection of one's past and a time to ponder one's future.

37 years ago today, God blessed your family with a wonderful gift, a gift we have been privileged to enjoy as well. Your friendship has and always will be treasured, your unwavering loyalty unquestioned, your strength and conviction beyond reproach.

One could never choose a better companion or confidante than you. Through your most simple actions you constantly redefine honor, courage and dignity.

With love always,
Keri and Jim

Keri actually found the card by accident, although *I don't really believe in accidents*. Everything is interconnected, and it's up to us to see the relevance of what is before us. Keri also discovered the letter that our then eight-year-old daughter Amanda wrote about her "uncle" Josh. She was clearly feeling the same sense of loss that we felt; yet even this young child saw the blessings before her:

I'd like to dedicate this to my uncle Josh and I really miss him. He died last year at the age of 37. He died of a blood disease. After he died my dad was really upset because he was great friends with him.

The things I know about him is that his house was bigger than a Motel. He liked to shave his head. He liked to wear baseball caps. I think that's how come I like to wear caps. (Amanda wore a baseball cap almost every day until she became a teenager.)

I knew him since I was born. Even though I loved him, I didn't get to see him much. When he died I was around 7 1/2 or 8. He died in his bed. I really miss him but I know he's watching over me.

I believe Josh *was* watching over all of us. My card was stored in a box along with other keepsakes under our bed. Amanda's letter was hidden in the back of our bedroom dresser drawer. It was just another in a series of events that led me to believe he was really still with me.

Before Josh died he gave me a gift—one of his favorite jackets, a well-worn leather motorcycle jacket. At the time, neither of us rode a bike, but he loved the way it looked, and so did I. Josh was four-inches taller, and his shoulders were considerably broader than mine, so without even trying it on, I knew the jacket would be far too large for me. But I took it happily because he wanted me to have it.

After he died, that jacket sat in our hallway closet for a year before I ever tried it on.

One night, I was meeting some friends, and I told my wife that I finally decided to wear Josh's jacket. While I was out, I put my wallet in one of its many pockets. In another pocket, I found something amazing—fifteen crisp one-hundred-dollar bills. Coincidentally, earlier that day, we had received a bill for Carly's private school. It was a bill that we frankly did not know how we were going to pay. Josh was proud to be Carly's Godfather. When I got home Keri was sound asleep. I woke her by jumping on our bed and throwing the money into the air all around her.

I was convinced then, as I am now, that the money was a gift from Josh, which he intended for us to discover when we needed it most. I think that finding that last birthday card was no mere coincidence, any more than finding that money in that jacket pocket was an accident. Our friendship endures. Thanks again, old friend.

> **"To the soul, there is hardly anything more healing than friendship."**
> —Thomas Moore (1779-1852)

THE TRAVELING JACKET

Several years after Josh passed away, I met Greg. We traveled together to the Cannes Film Festival while on assignment for CNN. He also worked for the network. We lived on opposite coasts. Greg had the kind of confidence and swagger that only comes from growing up in New York City. I knew within minutes of meeting him that I liked him.

During our trip, Greg spoke with enthusiasm about riding his beloved Harley-Davidson motorcycle. When we returned home from our weeklong excursion, and I discovered that his fortieth birthday was fast approaching, I knew exactly what to give him. I packed up that worn leather jacket I had received from Josh and sent it to Greg as his birthday present. Like Josh, Greg was tall and broad shouldered, and I knew it would look great on him. That jacket, of course, had been very special to me. But it wasn't ever really mine. I was simply its custodian. Josh gave it to me, I believe, as a way to watch over me. He knew the jacket would not fit, but he also knew that I would discover the money hidden in the pocket. Josh's jacket had brought me luck. I hoped it would bring more of the same to my new friend, Greg. I know that Josh would have approved. A part of Josh now touched someone he never even met.

Greg loved the jacket, just as I knew that he would. He also appreciated the story behind it.

To honor one's friends, we must first identify them and embrace them. Let them know how you feel. Don't assume they already know. Who are the few people you can really count as *your* friends? Have you made sure they know how you feel about them? It's my new mission. Time is wasting.

GRATITUDE

"For today and its blessings,
I owe the world an attitude of gratitude."
—Clarence E. Hodges

IT'S TOO EASY TO OVERLOOK BLESSINGS, BOTH SMALL AND LARGE. I know I have done that far too many times in my life. When things are going well, it's easy to take those bounties for granted. My wife Keri and I had two beautiful daughters, Carly and Amanda who were just three and six when Keri got pregnant again. This time, our baby was going to be a boy.

Naming him became a family project. For a time, Oliver was in the lead, but we finally thought of the perfect name from all of us—it was going to be "Jack"—a combination of Jim, Amanda, Carly and Keri. We were all excited and looking forward to having a new little guy to cherish.

Keri and I went together to several doctor's visits. After just a few weeks, we saw the baby's first ultrasound. Everything looked fine. Eventually, it was time to schedule Keri's amniocentesis. We got a call telling us the results were in, and we were instructed to visit the doctor to receive the results in person. We already had two healthy and adorable little girls, and we probably took it for granted that if we had another child, we could count on more of the same. We were wrong.

Intuitively, Keri already knew the news was bad. Her doctor was a dear man who had treated Keri for many years. He delivered both our daughters. He always showed Keri both compassion and care.

The test results could not have been worse. Our unborn son had hit what I called the super lotto of genetic bad news. He had an extreme case of spina bifida, a serious birth defect resulting in an incompletely formed spinal cord. This particular case showed a malformation high up the spine, guaranteeing irreversible quadriplegia. The fetus was also hydrocephalic, having an abnormally large head caused by the pressure of excess cerebrospinal fluid forcing the forming bones to bulge outward. The fetus, our child, did not survive. We were already told to expect the worse, but still, we were devastated—Keri most of all.

Keri is the most gentle, loving woman I have ever known. She is the kind of mom who could take away the pain of a child's scraped knee with her warm embrace and tender voice whispering in their ear, "It's okay, sweetheart. Mommy will make it better." This was a situation that mommy could *not* make better, and it wounded her deeply. The loss and anguish seemed, for a time, so profound that we all worried about Keri. We were also a family grieving for the loss of the baby we would never know.

Several years later, Keri was shocked and surprised when she became pregnant again. Our daughters were almost eight and eleven. Once more, it was a boy. What otherwise should have been a joyous occasion, reignited Keri's deep-seeded fears that another terrible nightmare was about to come true.

We were told that the likelihood of a genetic anomaly occurring again was much greater this time around, given that it had already happened once before. Plus, Keri was now thirty-nine, and the risks to both her and the child were significantly higher than they had been with either of our daughters. Keri was understandably terrified. It was, without a doubt, an almost unbearable experience for all of us.

Even after a series of tests confirmed the child was fine, Keri remained convinced that anything that *could* go wrong, *would* go wrong. She seemed to completely withdraw from those closest to her, and from the world around her, falling into a quiet depression. Keri's emotional defense was to ignore the pregnancy altogether. She refused to invest herself emotionally in a process that she believed would end badly. For months, we could not even address the fact that her stomach was growing with a new life inside. We were not allowed to talk about the baby or even bring up the subject of names. The loss of a child, years before, felt so present once again to Keri that her fears, no matter how unfounded, felt all too real.

The timing of his birth came as a surprise. One month before her due date, Keri went to the doctor for a checkup. He reassured her she had at least ten more days before our son would be born. I was supposed to catch a plane the next day for a brief trip to Memphis, Tennessee, to mark the twentieth anniversary of Elvis Presley's death at Graceland, so I was relieved to know we still had some time. It didn't turn out that way. That evening, as Keri and I watched a televised Fleetwood Mac concert, she knew things were happening too quickly. Her water broke—the only one of our children for whom this happened, and Keri felt severe cramps almost immediately. We called the doctor, and he said to meet him at the hospital right away. We had been through too much to take any chances.

Keri was anemic during her pregnancy, and when she was given medication for pain, her blood pressure suddenly dipped to a dangerously low level. I could see the look of concern on the nurse's face as she tended to Keri, who had nearly passed out by this point. Our daughters were kept in another room with their grandparents, unaware of the situation, while the medical team worked to get the heart rates of both Keri and our unborn baby within normal limits. After all Keri had been through with this pregnancy and having suffered so deeply by losing our last baby, I could not bear to think of anything going wrong now. I held Keri's hand as I saw the terror on her face when she realized she never felt like this during either of our daughters' births. But this time, the nightmare of that earlier failed pregnancy would not haunt us again. This child was more of a fighter than we could imagine. After several minutes, which seemed more like hours, everything was once again under control. Keri's blood pressure returned to normal, and the baby monitor revealed that our son was fine as well.

When our son was finally born, he was completely healthy. We named him Matthew, which means gift from God, because that is, in fact, what he was. Matthew is now eleven years old. To this day, he remains our heavenly gift. Keri still looks at him and marvels over his perfect back and his beautiful face. There is not a day that goes by that both Keri and I don't give thanks for the blessing of all three of our children. They are happy, thriving, wonderful individuals. We don't take anything for granted, not the least of which, the fact that they are all healthy.

> **"Don't it always seem to go, that you**
> **don't know what you've got till it's gone."**
> —Joni Mitchell

I didn't realize it fully then, but I do now.

At a time when I am questioning the value of life itself, I appreciate the joys I already have in front of me. I promised myself that I would begin making a "gratitude list." My new daily ritual consisted of noting those things for which I was truly grateful in my life—my family, my friends past and present, my health, and the opportunities I have been given. The more I practiced, the easier it became. Not just to *say* it. To *own* it with conviction. To believe it.

No matter where you are in your life, there are things that are truly blessings—count them and cherish them *before* they are gone.

LOVE

> "All you need is love."
> —John Lennon (1940-1980)

LOVE—OVERRATED IN SONGS? PERHAPS, UNDERRATED IN DAILY LIFE? REGRETTABLY. I am convinced that there is no power greater than love to inspire, comfort, elevate, heal and define the human spirit.

I think of my love for my parents, who sacrificed for me and made sure I had every opportunity they never had. My wife struggled with me, pushed me, inspired me and always believed in me, even those times I did not believe in myself. My children have loved me unconditionally and taught me that the *more you love, the more capacity you have to love.*

As important as love is the *expression* of love both in words and in actions. I have always been somewhat of a hopeless romantic, to the point of being accused of being overly sappy. I always tell the people I love that I love them. I try to show it as well, not with *presents* but through my *presence*, demonstrating thoughtfulness and love in the simplest acts of kindness and tenderness. Long after gifts are forgotten, the impact of true love endures. I end phone conversations with my parents, my wife, my children the same way—"I love you."

> **"And in the end, the love you take**
> **is equal to the love you make."**
> —Paul McCartney

HOLLY

When I was nine years old, I witnessed an act of selflessness and love that I could not really appreciate until many years later.

It was the summer of 1966, and I was away for a month at a camp not far from our home in Los Angeles. My mom, Gloria, had married Gery three years before. Though he was technically my step-dad, I called him "dad" from the beginning.

On parents' day, Gery came to visit me at camp, but my mom was not with him. He told me that she was in the hospital and was not well enough to come, but that she would be fine. He said she'd be home when camp was over in two more weeks. Out of the blue, he then asked how I felt about having a sibling. I thought about it for a moment and said that I would love to have a baby *brother* but that I did not want a *sister. I wanted a brother to play catch and ride bikes with. I was nine and my vision of a perfect world did not yet include girls.* I didn't realize how disappointed my answer made Gery. My mom, who was only twenty-six at the time, had been looking forward to having more children with

Gery. Unbeknownst to me, she was rushed to the hospital while I was at camp to remove several grapefruit-sized fibroid tumors which had grown in her abdomen. Thankfully, it turned out that the growths were not malignant, but they still had to be removed. While my mom was in surgery, the doctor concluded it was necessary to perform a partial hysterectomy. My mom didn't find out until it was too late. When she awoke from the anesthesia in the recovery room, Gery was by her side, telling her everything went well and that she would be fine. The first question she asked him was, "Can we still have a child?" My dad told her, "Yes."

Soon after, when my mom discovered what had happened in the operating room, she became enraged, hurt and tearful. "How could you lie to me?" she asked my dad. "I had a hysterectomy! You told me we could have a baby!"

"We can, and we do," replied my dad. "We have a daughter."

As it turns out, three hours before the surgeon performed my mom's hysterectomy, he had also delivered a baby to an unmarried fifteen-year-old girl. That teenaged mom knew she would give the infant up for adoption, but she had not made any decisions beyond that. While my mom was in recovery, the doctor said to my dad, "You two are so young, you can always adopt a baby in the future. In fact, I just delivered a baby girl, and the parents aren't keeping her." My dad replied without skipping a beat, "How do we get the baby?" The doctor immediately went to the new mother's room and spoke with her and her family. He explained that he knew a young couple no longer able to have a child of their own naturally, but were eager to adopt this beautiful baby girl of theirs. He continued that this couple already had a son and would provide a loving home for their newborn girl. Clearly, the doctor had a good relationship with this teenaged mom and her family, and they trusted his instincts to allow the baby to go to my folks. That day, my dad visited the maternity ward and looked through the glass, gazing for the first time on the little girl who would become his daughter.

My dad hired a lawyer, as did the other family, and all the proper documents were quickly drafted and signed. Two weeks later, my dad drove to the lawyer's office and picked up the newborn girl, swaddled in a blanket for the first trip to her new home. My mom had only been out of the hospital for a few days herself. Her recovery from the extensive abdominal surgery would prove to be fairly lengthy, but now she had a new reason to regain her strength as quickly as possible. While she was resting in the hospital bed temporarily set up in the living room of their two-story home, my dad walked through the front door and introduced my mom to her daughter. It was the first time mom had ever seen her. They named her Holly.

In the span of a month, my mom had a hysterectomy, my parents adopted a baby girl, and they moved into their first home. My folks were young, both in their mid-twenties. Their newly- built house, which they bought for just under $50,000 in the hills above Los Angeles, had a mortgage payment of $249 a month. That was a lot of money for them at the time. In fact, they decided against installing a pool while the house was being built because it would have increased the payment by $10 a month. The hospital bill for my sister's delivery came to $1,500, which, for them, might as well have been $150,000. Still, they paid using up virtually all their remaining savings. My parents had friends who were also trying to adopt a child. Some of them had already waited for two years or more to find a baby. Somehow, my dad arranged the whole thing in a matter of days. *While I do not necessarily believe in fate, I am often convinced that there are no accidents.*

When I returned home from camp, we were now a family of four. I had a new baby sister. Despite my initial objections, Holly quickly became my favorite little person in the world. My parents may have adopted Holly, but my friends and I soon claimed her as our own official mascot of the neighborhood. Adopting Holly took a single act of love, and it changed all our lives in an instant. Holly is now a mother herself, but she will always be my baby sister.

> **"To love is to receive a glimpse of heaven."**
> —Karen Sunde

BROTHERLY LOVE

When my brother Christian was just a toddler, he was never able to pronounce his own name. It always came out sounding like "Chicken."

Eventually, of course, that became his nickname. Even as an adult, when my children or I refer to him, it's either as "Chris," "Chick" or "Chicken." It is always accepted in the spirit in which it is intended, as an endearment.

Chick and I have the same father, but we grew up in different homes, to different mothers. We are more than half brothers; we are blood brothers. By the time he was ten and I was thirteen, we were legally separated by my adoption to Gery. We were no longer joined in name or by law. But no distance, legal or physical, could break the emotional bonds that had been forged since early childhood. I was, and remain, his big brother.

In some ways he was the Lex Luther to my Clark Kent. Our lives and our reactions to just about everything were polar opposites. My method of dealing with my childhood traumas was, I suspect quite subconsciously, to become the perfect child. Gloria and Gery jokingly say that they are still waiting for me to do something wrong. I had committed myself to excel at everything. At summer camp, I earned the Best Camper award four years in a row. I won the American Legion Award in the ninth grade; I was elected Student Body President in middle school. In high school I was the star of the two senior plays, a letterman in track, a member of the student senate and a straight-A student.

Chicken took a markedly different approach. He was the angry rebel, and he was often in trouble. By the time he was in his mid-teens he was already drowning himself in alcohol and trying any drug that was available. Temper and violence were the temporary salves to his emotional wounds. His journey of self-destruction proved nearly fatal on so many occasions that it became almost commonplace, and sadly, expected.

Through it all, we spent relatively few days together, and yet, those memories remain most sacred and vivid for each of us. We were so different, and yet, we identified so strongly with one another. He has joked on more than one occasion that if you combined our talents and personalities, we could rule the world. I suppose through it all, we remained uniquely capable of understanding without judging one another. Our conversations, while only occasional, dealt with intense topics, both emotional and intellectual, and the inevitable hour to two-hour sessions left us both exhilarated and exhausted, in much the same way an incredible meal leaves you tired and full, but completely satisfied.

In his twenties, Chicken learned to channel his rage and anger onto the page as a writer. The honesty and intensity of his work was financially rewarding. More importantly, his books and screenplays were masterful and humbling. At times, I feared that I could not distinguish between the autobiographical and imaginary portions of his work. He confided in me that he chose fiction as his outlet because writing the truth with complete honesty would only result in hurting those people closest to him. It was his cathartic release. It has served him well. In addition to creating some of the most riveting and disturbing characters and scenarios, he, somewhat ironically, also wrote the story for a charming animated film, which he intended as a love letter to our father.

For years, I was worried that Christian's self-destructive behavior could have only one possible outcome, and I had grown too accustomed to burying friends to even dare contemplate what it would be like to lose a brother. Chicken's salvation came in the most unlikely of places. Jenna and Quinn were the children of Chicken's dear old friend, who was, in fact, his former longtime girlfriend.

While their romance had long since fizzled, they remained close, and their friendship grew stronger. She got married and had two children before eventually divorcing. The children's father lived out of state, and while he remained a strong and loving influence in their lives, the distance created a void. While the children were still very young, my brother became very attached to them, and graciously, they, along with their mom, welcomed him into their family as a kind of surrogate uncle.

Chicken never married, and he had long since recognized the fact that he never would. He was almost proud of his hermit-like lifestyle, and he was also well aware of how difficult *he* could be to live with. While he has never, to my knowledge, been formally diagnosed with obsessive-compulsive disorder, I am certain he has it. In his home, everything has its place, down to the smallest of details. Even his toiletries are arranged at right angles and carefully spaced in drawers and on his bathroom counter. In his cupboards, all labels are uniformly adjusted to face out, and his expansive collections of books, movies and music are organized neatly and alphabetically.

Yet, these two children, at first Jenna and then Quinn, ignited a paternal instinct in this loner that I instantly recognized because I felt it with my own children. His time spent with them became a remarkable obsession of love and kindness. He read to them, cared for them, nurtured them and helped raise them. His life, once driven by chaos, now had a purpose. To this day he remains their legal guardian in the event anything happens to their mom. Chick is an incredibly talented writer, but he is an even better parent. That is a compliment he would be proud to accept.

Christian's selflessness with Jenna and Quinn had an amazingly positive and grounding influence on him. Through loving those children, Christian *healed himself,* filling the holes and emptiness in his own soul. Love had exorcised his demons. It is a remarkable thing. Jenna and Quinn, now both teenagers, continue to give direction to *Christian's* life, and he gives direction to *theirs,* not in a judgmental, threatening way, but with honesty, tenderness and understanding. The time and energy he invested has been repaid through their growth, academic achievements and through the confident, successful young adults they are becoming. His unwavering and unconditional love for them is returned tenfold.

Christian tells me that I am one of the first people, and the only member of his family, to recognize and embrace their significance to each other. On his refrigerator is a photo of me with Jenna, perhaps then only five years old. We were at a birthday party at a bowling alley, and we are standing in a lane. I am crouched down, and we are both smiling, cheek-to-cheek. After he took the picture, he says that I walked over to him and said, "Chick, I understand completely. How could you *not* fall in love with that beautiful little face?"

Salvation comes in many forms. For Chicken it came in the guise of two toddlers who helped him recapture lost innocence and joy and gave him a sense of fulfillment he had long since stopped trying to find outside his work. His love of those two children saved my brother.

> "There's always one who loves and
> one who lets himself be loved."
> —W. Somerset Maugham (1874-1965)

NICOLE

There are no accidents.

While I was writing about "*Love*," the telephone rang. A dear friend of mine called to say that a mutual friend, Nicole, a vibrant, contagiously optimistic young woman, had passed away overnight. She had been battling brain cancer for years. For a time, it looked like she had beaten it.

I met Nicole when she was working hard to become a news producer at CNN. There was no question that she would succeed. She had a laugh and a lilt in her chirpy voice that made her seem much younger than her twenty-three years. If her voice and ever-present smile didn't disarm you, her eyes would. They were a beautiful, vivid blue, and they revealed a purity of soul. My daughter Amanda was only eight when she met Nicole. Kids see kindness immediately. Amanda invited Nicole to those early birthday parties, and she always came ready to have fun. Nicole never lost her childlike spirit.

After her initial diagnosis, followed by terribly debilitating treatments, Nicole not only embraced life, she attacked it. She worked behind the scenes on two different national television programs. Her effusiveness was always reciprocated. You simply had no choice. Nicole overflowed with love, and it was impossible not to be touched by it.

In her last few days she suffered a sudden, and by all appearances, final setback. Nicole's last hours were not spent alone. Her friends and family gathered by her side, many clinging to the belief that even this most recent battle was not going to be her last. Not surprisingly, I am told that she died with a smile on her face. My deep regret was that I was not among those with Nicole letting her know how much she was loved. I had told her many times before, but this final opportunity is lost forever.

In your last hours, whom would you tell? Don't let the words go unsaid. Act as if each time you speak with someone it might be the *last* time you speak with him or her.

I made a list of the people beyond my immediate family who mean the most to me. I thought, "Who has had a positive impact on my life—big or small—and may not even know how I feel?" I imagined receiving a call from someone telling me how important I was to them—how I had changed their life in a meaningful way, and all they wanted to do was to make sure I knew. It would feel amazing, wouldn't it? I decided that it was time to start making those calls myself.

True love is the desire to give to another without asking or expecting anything in return. It is the placement of another's happiness above your own. Love is not something to take for granted. I don't.

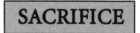

"The important thing is this: To be able at any moment to sacrifice what we are for what we could become."
—Charles DuBois (1804-1867)

"Sometimes when you sacrifice something precious, you're not really losing it.
You're just passing it on to someone else."
—Mitch Albom

BECOMING A DAD

WHEN MY MOM MARRIED GERY IN 1963, I WAS SIX AND A HALF YEARS OLD. He was twenty-six, and he made his living selling cars. He worked nights and weekends, the prime shifts for auto sales. My mom was working full time for a clothing manufacturer. I like to think that I was the draw in Gery asking my mom to marry him, but the fact is, no matter how cute I may have been, we hardly knew each other.

They married only a matter of weeks after meeting each other, and I suspect his family viewed them as impulsive and crazy to marry so quickly. They exchanged vows at a wedding chapel on Las Vegas Boulevard. It was a late-night ceremony. As my folks tell me, they awakened the Justice of the Peace and his wife, and she and the taxi driver were both witnesses. They recently celebrated their forty-fifth anniversary. Theirs was an almost instant attraction. Sometimes first impressions are right.

Gery quickly realized that if we were to become a *real* family, our relationship had to be based on more than time spent occasionally at the breakfast table. He made what I consider one of the more loving sacrifices in my life. He quit his job for six months so that he could spend virtually all his time with me. Even at twenty-six, Gery already knew what I wouldn't learn until my mid-forties, that *family always trumps career.* I had almost lost sight of that until it was too late. Gery made the same sacrifice that my mentor Tom convinced me to make with my own family. Gery's dramatic and selfless act enabled us to get to know one another, not as my mom's new husband, but as my step-dad.

I have always been uncomfortable with the term stepdad because it presupposes a "less than" status in a child's life, which, especially in Gery's case, I have always found unfair and undeserved. That's how I came to have two dads.

Those six months formed the basis for a lifetime of trust, love, guidance and selflessness that may never have been forged without Gery choosing to sacrifice short-term financial gain for long-term emotional stability. It was a priceless gift.

It may seem paradoxical, but I am convinced that often when you make a sacrifice, you actually get more than you give up. What sacrifices have you made in your own life that ultimately brought you more than they cost you? What do you value so much that you would gladly give up something, perhaps everything, in order to save it? It's never too late to prioritize.

> "Dedicate some of your life to others.
> Your dedication will not be a sacrifice.
> It will be an exhilarating experience because it is an
> intense effort applied toward a meaningful end."
> —Dr. Thomas Dooley (1927-1961)

FAMILY

I have lived in Los Angeles for my entire life. Remaining here was always very important to me and to my wife. Our parents live just five minutes away, and our three children still see them on an almost daily basis—what a gift both to our parents and to our kids!

Thanks to growing interest from rival networks, I was fortunate to negotiate a no-cut, no-move contract with CNN, where I worked as a news anchor from early 1992 to 2001. In simple terms, that meant that I could not be moved to another city without my consent, and if my bosses wanted to fire me, they had to pay me in full for the duration of my contract. At that time, I had over two years remaining on a three-year deal.

When I was summoned to Atlanta to meet with network executives in November 1999, I had no idea that I would be facing one of the most pivotal choices in my life. I was told that the Los Angeles bureau, where I had worked since being hired nearly a decade before, was being scaled back. The ill-fated AOL-Time Warner merger was still in its early stages, and there were massive cuts being ordered across the board at CNN. Production in the LA office was being reduced dramatically. The two programs I co-anchored were being cancelled. If I wanted to remain with the network, I had to relocate to Atlanta. I was offered the anchor job on CNN's two-hour morning newscast, based at the network's headquarters.

Under normal circumstances, I would have been able to cope with such a life-altering transition. But my situation at that point was anything but normal.

After seventeen years of marriage, my wife and I were having serious marital troubles, prompting us to separate a few weeks before. I was living near my family at a local hotel while we decided what to do.

Our story was not unusual but that made it no less painful. After a long, successful marriage, Keri and I had grown apart. For a time, we were strangers in the same home, not because we no longer loved one another but because we felt like we no longer knew one another. There is little doubt in my mind that our intimacy was strained and damaged during her pregnancy with Matthew. Keri was dealing with such turbulent emotions that she built an emotional wall around herself, not only from me but from our daughters as well. Keri was terrified, given the trauma of her previous pregnancy, and her reaction was completely understandable to me. But I had allowed myself to drift into my own shell as well. We had gone from lovers to little more than housemates, sharing only the love for our children.

The estrangement was certainly as much my fault. I was withdrawn and unhappy, and perhaps I had stopped trying and failed to see it until it was almost too late. I had long experienced tremendous difficulty expressing myself openly and honestly on a day-to-day basis.

How ironic that I made my living connecting with total strangers, making them feel comfortable enough to speak to me freely, and yet, I could not connect with my own wife.

The professional choice before me was something I was not prepared to consider. To take the assignment would have meant literally leaving my family. After all, how could I uproot my wife and our children when we were not even living together? To turn down the job meant I had to leave the network entirely, ending a career that had taken off, both in terms of responsibility and financial rewards.

I scheduled an appointment with the outgoing chairman of the network, Tom Johnson. He had become both a mentor and a trusted friend. I now needed his advice and guidance. Tom was a Southern gentleman in the truest sense of the word. He valued honesty and integrity, in a business being overrun by a tabloid, ratings-driven mentality. When I explained my situation he told me to sit down. Tom closed the door of his office, and he spoke to me calmly, yet forcefully, with candor and passion. He confided that in his professional life, he too had been forced to make difficult choices, and sometimes the ramifications of those decisions reverberated for years to come. To him, the decision before me was straightforward.

He said that at the end of my life, no one would care whether I hosted another show on CNN or any other network for that matter. I would ultimately be judged on my character and the kind of father, husband and person I had been. "If your marriage can be fixed," he said, "you have to go home and fix it, simple as that. The way I see it, we owe you two years pay, and we can't ask you to move if you don't want to. I am telling you that you don't want to." It was a verbal slap in the face that initially shocked me until I realized what a profound gift Tom had just given me. I had been handed a second chance to save my marriage and my family.

Tom made it clear that he would not allow me to consider accepting the reassignment. He knew that turning down the offer meant abruptly ending my career at CNN. But taking it would be, on a personal level, even more devastating. I went home with a new perspective on the choices before us.

Keri and I soon began seeing a counselor, a difficult but necessary step to take. I used to regard therapy as a sign of weakness, but I have come to appreciate it as a demonstration of courage—facing one's demons and challenges head on, rather than ignoring them at any cost. We needed to work through our estrangement *together* and see if our relationship could be saved, if it could endure and grow. We decided that we could not face one another, let alone our children and families, with the prospect of divorce unless we could first say that we tried everything possible to save our marriage. The process was gut wrenching. I began to see and appreciate the love and history we shared with one another, not to mention our three beautiful children who needed and deserved to have two parents committed to them, as well as to each other.

Sacrifices routinely must be made in everyone's life. This time, my career had to be sacrificed for the benefit of my family. So much of my identity had been wrapped up in what I did for a living that it was a profound loss to voluntarily leave my professional home behind, not knowing what impact it might have on my future. I knew almost immediately that the effort was well spent. It was worth the price. Keri and I recently celebrated our twenty-seventh anniversary, and I believe we are both happier today than we were twenty years ago.

Was it a worthwhile sacrifice to choose my family over my career? You bet it was. I have since thanked Tom for his graciousness and generosity. I will remain grateful to him for the rest of my life.

COMMITMENT

"Let us be grateful to people who make
us happy: They are the charming gardeners
who make our souls blossom."
—Marcel Proust (1871-1922)

OUR HARD WORK PAID OFF.

Keri and I not only began talking again, we were actually listening and understanding one another. We enjoyed a renewed commitment to each other and to our family. Once our marriage was back on track, I decided that Keri deserved a very public reaffirmation of my love for her on our twentieth anniversary. Our oldest daughter, Amanda, and I secretly planned a surprise wedding to mark the occasion. I booked a beautiful dining room and outdoor patio at one of our favorite hotels, The Peninsula in Beverly Hills. I hired a Beatles tribute band (the Beatles remain my favorite band), and I invited fifty family members and friends to witness and celebrate the retaking of our vows. I enlisted one of our oldest friends, Mindy, a talented wedding planner, to help with everything from flowers to food to photography. I was twenty-five when we first got married, and I admit that

I was not terribly involved in most of the decisions (except for choosing the cake). This time, I wanted to say (again) that, without question or hesitation, *Keri* was the woman I wanted to spend the rest of my life with.

Amanda relished her role as my co-conspirator in this loving deception. The ruse was easier to pull off than either of us had expected. I sent Keri and our daughters to have their hair cut for a special dinner at the hotel's five-star restaurant as guests of Keri's parents. We had eaten there before, and it seemed a logical venue to celebrate the evening. I had bought Keri a special dress just for the occasion, which again, was not all that unusual. I have a reputation among Keri's friends as being the ultimate metrosexual, since I usually buy all her purses and jewelry without any assistance from family or friends.

We arrived at the restaurant, and the Maitre d' followed the script perfectly, apologizing to Keri and her parents because our table was not yet ready. They offered us cocktails while we waited, but I suggested that we walk along the corridor and window shop at some of the hotel's stores. I was stunned to see one of our closest friends, and a guest at the party, standing in the hallway holding a gift. Seeing him threatened to ruin the entire surprise. Amanda silently motioned for him to quickly turn around, which he did. In retrospect, it must have looked ridiculous to see a grown man holding a present, staring directly at a wall, standing only inches away. Incredibly, Keri didn't notice a thing. When we got to the end of the hall, our guests, who were hiding around the corner, revealed themselves and shouted "surprise" in unison.

I escorted my now-crying wife to the courtyard. That's when she realized the full intent of my plan. There, a rabbi was waiting, standing beneath a beautiful floral canopy, laced with deep green vines and draped with cream roses. I reached into my jacket pocket and took out a small black velvet box. Opening it revealed a simple platinum band; its underside inscribed, "Jim loves Keri." Aside from the engraving, which was hidden from view once it was resting on her finger, the ring was completely unadorned, save for the polished ridge on each edge of the pillow-shaped band. It was the most precious piece of jewelry I had ever given her.

I got down on one knee, and, in front of our guests, I asked her, "Will you marry me...again?" I had never properly proposed twenty years before, and this was my chance to do it right, this time with an audience. Through her tears, Keri was almost unable to speak, but I knew from her broad smile that the answer was "yes."

The ceremony was brief but heartfelt. It was already the most meaningful night of my life. As she did at our first wedding, Keri cried through our vows. She has always been so charmingly sentimental. It's one of her many endearing qualities. In our second wedding the vows had a new and greater significance. Our youthful idealism was tempered with the wisdom that only experience can bring. We knew firsthand the implication and true meaning of "for better or for worse, for richer or poorer." After we said, "I do," we were officially reintroduced as husband and wife. We kissed tenderly before all the people who were most important to us.

I made a brief speech before heading into the party that followed. I told everyone that the reason I had planned this elaborate surprise was simple: Keri and I had been through a trying period in our marriage, a test of the heart, and we had made it through, together. For a time, I did not know if we would reach our seventeenth anniversary, but now I knew that we could easily enjoy our fiftieth and beyond. I was so proud to publicly reaffirm our commitment to one another.

It was a magical and romantic night. I will never forget it. This time, the people most important to us in the world, the ones who literally personified our union and our love, our three children, were present for the joyous night. The "Beatles" played three sets—one as the early Beatles, one from the "Rubber Soul" era, and finally as "Sgt. Pepper's Lonely Hearts Club Band." I played guitar with the band and sang "And I Love Her" to my wife in front of all our closest family and friends. It was perfect.

Was it extravagant and over the top? Absolutely, and it was worth every penny. My wife and I had been through an emotional hell, and we had both chosen to recommit to one another. It didn't simply happen. *Waiting or hoping* for something to happen would have been a death sentence to our marriage. We made the conscious pledge to one another to ensure that something happened. We had also fallen in love again. We know that we have a future together, but just as important, we share a loving, rich past, a sense of history that can never be replaced. *It took almost losing everything to make me realize what I really wanted to keep, at almost any cost.*

"Passion is the quickest to develop and
the quickest to fade. Intimacy develops more slowly,
and commitment more gradually still."
—Robert Sternberg

RANDY

I met Randy a few months after I began dating his sister, who eventually became my wife. Randy was twenty-four. He lived large, and his dreams were even bigger. Home for Randy was Los Angeles, but he routinely flew to the east coast on Fridays to spend the weekend with his girlfriend who lived in Boston. Randy had never finished college, but he found early success in the garment industry, much like his father before him.

While still in his twenties, Randy met the woman who would ultimately change his life. His courtship with Barbara was brief but intense, and, within a few months, they married in a simple ceremony in Los Angeles. Soon after, Randy started his first company with a partner, manufacturing clothes in the LA garment district. It looked like their future was going to be bright. Neither of them knew at the time that Randy's health had already begun its silent and steady downward spiral. Recently, Keri and I found some photos of Randy taken around that time. His bright eyes and confident smile were shocking reminders of how happy and more importantly, how healthy, he had once been.

Randy's loss of balance and constant fatigue were the first indications that something was wrong. Next, lapses with his memory and speech revealed this was more serious than anyone had first expected. Through a series of tests and examinations, his doctors determined that Randy was suffering from the early stages of multiple sclerosis, a degenerative auto-immune disease for which there is no known cure, nor a meaningful treatment.

As Randy's illness progressed, it stole his ability to walk and corrupted his fine motor skills. It sapped his energy. He spent the early months of his illness traveling the world, trying experimental treatments and medications, to little or no avail. The insidious disease continues to take more and more of my brother-in-law every day.

Eventually, most of his time was spent confined to bed. Moving about his home requires significant help just to lift him into his electric wheelchair. His appearances at family dinners are less and less frequent. Leaving home just takes too much out of him. Even the simplest of activities have become monumental tasks.

Incredibly, the disease has not laid claim to Randy's offbeat sense of humor that first attracted Barbara to him. In spite of his challenges, Randy still surprises Barbara with his ability to make her laugh. That has proven her sole respite. They have remained married for more than twenty years, and together they raised a daughter. Barbara is both determined and devoted, and she continues to honor her vows to stay with Randy *for better or for worse*. Through strength, sheer will and constant commitment she has single-handedly held their small family together.

If this were my last day, I decided I had better be engaged and invested in everything I have left to do. I made a list of the things, principles and people to which I was committed. It's a valuable list to make, no matter how long you have left.

If you had to truly commit to any people, principles or plans—what would they be? Are you willing to place those commitments above everything else? After all, isn't that what commitment is all about?

FORGIVENESS

"The weak can never forgive.
Forgiveness is the attribute of the strong."
—Mahatma Gandhi (1869-1948)

FOR ME, FORGIVENESS IS MORE OF A PROCESS THAN A SINGLE ACT. It involves ending feelings of resentment or anger against another person who either hurt you or whom you believe hurt you. Most important, it also involves doing so without demanding punishment or retribution. Apology requires caring and humility. Forgiveness can be even more challenging.

Forgiveness is liberating. Anger and resentment are emotional shackles that choke your soul. Freeing yourself from these negative feelings opens you up to experiencing joys you simply overlook.

This area of self-examination was by far the most daunting undertaking of the entire challenge, almost as difficult as imagining that I had one day left to live. It involves the people closest and dearest to me, and it is bound to upset all of them. I did not write from a place of blame or anger, but with understanding and forgiveness. *That was my ultimate epiphany and my salvation.*

My parents were teenagers when they married and when I was born. They divorced when I was less than two years old. My father remarried, and my half-brother Christian was born a short time later. My second half-brother, Anthony, arrived a few years later.

It was a struggle for my mom to raise me alone, and the anger she felt toward my father for leaving us and remarrying was obvious. She used scissors to literally cut my father out of all our family photos in an apparent effort to eliminate him from our lives. But she couldn't eliminate him completely because of who he was.

In 1959, as the star of *Gidget*, playing the role of Moondoggie, James Darren became one of the first all-American idols. For most of my life it has been the elephant in the room—with my friends, in my professional life and especially with my family. When you divorce a celebrity, they never really go away. There is a constant reminder on television, radio and movie marquees that, not only are they still around, they are adored by millions of others.

It has always been clear to me that my parents were incompatible, but without their intense and turbulent relationship I would not be here. Still, the split produced extreme bitterness on both sides. Those sore feelings continue to this day. Into my adolescence, I continued to see my biological father every other weekend and for a month each summer, but the relationship between my parents was seldom civil.

I have always called and considered Gery my dad, but I also had a father-son relationship with my biological father. I actually called them both "dad" although in order to distinguish between the two in conversation, I generally referred to James as my father and Gery as my dad. It's hard to have two dads, and I've always been mindful that both are painfully aware that the other man is such an important figure in my life.

My father's second wife, Evy, was always warm and loving toward me. She always asked that I call her by her first name, but it was clear that she always viewed me as part of her family.

My father was not *born* James Darren, he *became* James Darren. As a child, he was James William Eroclani. As his first-born son, I was named James William Ercolani Jr.

My father, Evy, and my brothers Christian and Anthony, all took the last name of Darren. How ironic that I was the only member of my immediate family with the last name Ercolani. Meanwhile, my mom Gloria, Gery and Holly had the last name of Moret. It now almost seems funny, but it was hardly amusing to me at the time. *In name only, but significant nonetheless, I was in fact, alone.*

The humor, at least in retrospect, came in the constant battle between Gloria Moret and James Darren to change my last name to match theirs. In grammar school, in 5th and 6th grade, I was James Moret. In years 7, 8 and 9, I was James Ercolani Jr. In high school and beyond I was James Moret again. I suppose I can honestly claim that James Moret *never* attended middle school.

When I was perhaps ten or eleven years old, my father gave me a gold ring that bore the initials, "JD." My mom threw a fit when I returned home wearing it, saying, "That's not *his* real last name, and it's not *yours*, either." Following my mother's objections, my father had the ring changed to "JE," to reflect my birth name. Later, my mom took the ring and had the initials changed to "JM" for James Moret. At that point, my father was the one who went ballistic, taking the ring from me and changing the initials once again. And so it went. It was eventually changed once more to "JM."

Before I got married, I gave that ring to a jeweler and asked him to melt it down for the gold. I hated that ring and I never wanted to see it again. The thought of it still gives me a stomachache.

ADOPTION

Shortly after I turned thirteen, Gloria and James, who had been fighting over visitation, child support and even my last name, came up with an abrupt and shocking solution: Gery would legally adopt me. Perhaps, in my father's mind, this would finally stop the endless bickering with my mom. From what I remember about that time, my father was going through a particularly difficult period in his life. His television series, *The Time Tunnel,* had been cancelled a few years earlier, and he had not worked in some time. He was being advised by his business manager to sell his home and rent a house instead. I certainly don't presuppose that the agreement was made over financial considerations, only that it was an emotionally difficult time for him.

I don't know if I will ever fully understand how the deal for my adoption was struck. We all filter our memories through our own perceptions, and my mother and father are each particularly partisan. Time does little to add clarity to the events surrounding the decision. I was put in an extremely uncomfortable position. I was asked to choose one man over the other. They were the two most important men in my life. It was an impossible task. I was frightened and angry to be asked to make such a monumental and final decision. Despite the constant tug of war between Gloria and James, which had dogged me since childhood, James was still my father. But Gery was my dad. I was forever bound to each of them, one by nature, the other by nurture and to both of them by love. I physically resembled one, and so many of my beliefs and values were shaped by the other. How could I choose? I was just thirteen, and I was dealing with so many changes within my own body. Everything around me was new and confusing. *Divorces are always painful, but for the child in the middle they can be devastating.* I agreed to the adoption.

I remember sitting in the judge's chambers in Los Angeles Family Court, when the judge showed me my new birth certificate. As far as I knew, the old one no longer existed and neither did any mention of James Darren or James Ercolani on the new legal document placed before me. It was as if he never existed. My identity had literally and irrevocably been officially changed. I vividly recall leaving the courthouse and walking across the street, feeling lost and disillusioned. I had only been in chambers for a short time, but everything was somehow different once I left. I had a new last name. A part of me was gone forever.

My ties to James, Evy, Christian and Anthony remained in my heart but no longer existed in any legal sense. It was and continues to be a defining event in my life. It evoked feelings of confusion and loss. I believe it reinforced my deep desire to be liked and accepted, which motivates so much of what I do to this day.

The difficulty was compounded by the fact that long after the adoption, everyone who knew me also knew the identity of my father. To this day, a Google search of either of our names will eventually cross reference both of us. We are not bound in name but by truth and by blood. His influence on my life is as undeniable as it is unavoidable.

When I was in the twelfth grade, long after the adoption, someone ran up to me in the hall at school and shouted, "Your dad's dead! I just heard it on the radio!" As it turned out, it was singer Bobby Darin who had died of heart disease, not James Darren. That was years before the age of the Internet and instant information, and I still remember the minutes (which seemed like hours) of panic and shock until I was able to get to a pay phone and finally discovered the mistake.

For years I ignored the pain of the adoption and glossed over the memories, telling myself it was too long ago to still matter. I had, after all, long since reconciled with my father. We don't often talk about the adoption, but I suspect it is never far from either of our minds. I continue to have a loving relationship with him, his wife and my brothers, just as I continue to have a wonderful, loving relationship with my mom and dad.

Those feelings toward my father don't diminish the commitment and sacrifice Gery made in my life or in the love we share for each other. *It's not now nor ever was a competition between these two men.* Incredibly, as if I were being tested even further to choose between them, they both share the same birth date—June 8. They were born one year apart—to the day.

I once joked with my mom and asked if she checked resumes and birthdates before getting married. That, of course, meant that on Gery's and James' birthday, each of them knew that when I was not with one, I was most likely with the other. Of course, round two in this ongoing emotional tug of war always came about a week later on the calendar — *Father's Day.*

I know that James deeply regrets the adoption, and I can still see it haunting and tormenting him all these years later. Our relationship as father and son has transcended the legalities and now centers on the emotional and biological bonds that continue to bind us. I have lived through the pain, and I choose to focus now on the joy we share together. It is a complex relationship but one that I cherish.

My father and I have had several heart-to-heart discussions, and he has told me repeatedly that allowing me to be adopted was the single greatest mistake of his life. I believe him. I can't change the past. Some actions just can't be undone. Instead, I had to come to terms with the past. That was not a quick or easy process. For years I had focused on my feelings of abandonment, and I often questioned how this could have happened. Was it something I had done which prompted my father to give me up for adoption? Was it my fault that I did not do anything to block it? I realized that before moving forward, first, I had to let go of the past. I couldn't do anything to change it, so I decided to accept it instead. *Ultimately, I had to find peace through forgiveness.*

That forgiveness had to extend beyond my father's actions. I ultimately also had to forgive my mom for asking me to choose sides in a battle that needed to end with a truce rather than with a casualty. I choose not to take sides. I suspect it was too difficult for my parents to fully recognize that this wasn't a contest. There is no need to declare a winner or a loser. I can love without keeping score.

All of us make mistakes, both big and small. I made some pretty big mistakes in my own life, not the least of which was nearly losing my wife and family. It is far too easy to sit in judgment of others, but no good really comes of it. On the last day of my life, what good could possibly come from continuing to harbor anger or resentment? I can't imagine a better time to finally and completely let go of such feelings.

Aren't there people in your life who may deserve your forgiveness? Who are they? What have they done to hurt you? Isn't holding onto those feelings hurting *you* even more? Harboring resentment and pain is such a destructive force in life, and it takes so much more energy to keep it contained rather than letting it loose and setting it free. For me, the act of forgiveness almost felt as if I was finally able to exhale after holding my breath for decades. It has enabled me to build a relationship with my father as well as with my mom and dad free of guilt, and free of anger. That's what forgiveness did for me.

APOLOGY

> "Never apologize for showing feeling.
> When you do so, you apologize for truth."
> —Benjamin Disraeli (1804-1881)

DON'T BE TOO PROUD TO APOLOGIZE. Each of us is guilty of this.

Like most of us (probably all of us) I have said and done some stupid and even hurtful things. Sometimes, I have recognized those mistakes immediately, and other times they have not become apparent until months, or even years, later. Once I recognized them, however, I knew that I had a decision to make: ignore the transgression or do something about it. Remember that doing nothing is really choosing to allow the hurt to continue.

MY PERSONAL APOLOGY

My adoption was finalized several months shy of my fourteenth birthday. With the stroke of a judge's pen, my relationship with my father, his wife and my two brothers was officially deemed "over." Even though it went unsaid, *I was never to see them again.* I was also cut off from my father's parents, both of whom were still living on the east coast. Despite our legal separation, my father's family lived only a few miles away from me. I knew that it would only be a matter of time before we might run into one another. That day finally arrived over a year later.

One weekend, I remember riding my bike—my beloved Schwinn Sting Ray—and I saw my brother walking out of a local toy store. This particular store happened to be a favorite hangout for both of us. Christian was now twelve years old, and I couldn't believe how much he had grown since we last saw each other. I was simultaneously sad and excited. I hugged him and we spoke, awkwardly at first, until we each realized how happy we were to see one another again. How ironic that adopting my sister Holly *created* a family while *my* adoption *tore* one apart. Similar acts but dramatically different results.

Within a few minutes, I was stunned to discover how much had changed since the adoption. Chris and *his* family had moved. They were still in the same city, but amazingly, I had no idea where they now lived. It felt like a double blow to my chest. I had once been a part of that family. Now I was, in fact, a stranger. Chris invited me to follow him home and come visit our father.

I remember seeing Christian that day as clearly as if it was yesterday, but surprisingly, I have virtually no recollection of that reunion with my father. I do know that on that day my father and I formed a *pact* to begin seeing one another again in secret. I was now part of a clandestine plan to resurrect the very relationship that he legally relinquished. To make these meetings a reality required a high level of trickery. I enlisted friends to cover for me in the event I had to account for time spent with my father. Lying to Gloria and Gery became easier over time, but it was never guilt-free. I hated the deceit.

Within a couple of years, it simply became too big a burden to allow the fraud to continue. I also felt mad that I had to resort to such deception to continue a relationship I should never have been asked to give up. I finally admitted the charade to my mom and dad. I still remember her tears, my guilt, her feelings of betrayal and my shame, not so much for seeing my father or my brothers, but for the overwhelming need to hide it.

For years, it amazed and confounded me how Christian and my mother were on such good terms. She was always gracious and loving toward him, and those feelings were clearly mutual. Chris was also a fan and supporter of Gery's. "He is like a Bob Newhart character," he told me recently. "He is still and calm like a large lake, but ever so deep." Christian also innately understood that my love and devotion to my mom was based, in large part, on her unwavering devotion to me. She had dedicated her life to me. Their shared empathy actually enabled Christian and my mom to forge their own positive, strong relationship.

For a time, my sister Holly and Christian actually became close friends. I joked with both of them that I secretly wanted them to fall in love and marry, if only for the comedy of attending their wedding ceremony. I imagined seeing my mother and father reluctantly rejoined in a perverted Seinfeld-like plot that was at once misguided and hysterical. Thankfully, that never happened.

As a grown man with three children of my own, I have often wondered why I still allowed myself to relive the guilt and anguish of my own childhood. Why did I still worry about what each of my parents thought? I still felt trapped in the middle of their futile battle. The simple truth was so obvious that it had been all but invisible to me all this time. I had to *apologize to myself* and to *forgive myself* for the years of lying and worrying about how everyone else felt.

As it turns out, I finally realized that I didn't need to be perfect then, and I don't need to be perfect now. It's an impossible goal anyway. I only need to be honest, especially with myself.

For so long, I felt the need to apologize to my parents for lying. I no longer do. I am sad that I was in a position where I felt I had to deceive them, but there is no remorse and no regret in loving. I apologize to myself alone.

I forgive myself.

"Sorry seems to be the hardest word."
—Bernie Taupin

BABETTE

Broadcast news is a lot like the entertainment business. News personalities, or "infotainers" as I call them, suffer from an over-reliance on popularity and a dependence on ratings to survive. Agents represent reporters and anchors and negotiate their contracts and move them from one job to another. We form close personal relationships with our agents. They do more than get us work. They are our confidants, our psychologists and sometimes our friends. Babette and Kenny became my agents in 1990. Together, they helped guide my career to great success. When Babette and Kenny parted company in the late 1990s I remained with Kenny as my sole representative. I was contractually bound to remain with him, but it was difficult to lose the other half of the team which had guided me. Babette and I remained close, and to her credit she never once tried to woo me away from Kenny. Still, she always let me know that she was available if I needed her.

When I left CNN, I began to rely on Kenny to a point where I actually lost my sense of direction and self. I went from *doing* to *waiting*—waiting for the phone to ring, waiting for a job offer. Offers never came. Perhaps I was aiming too high. As I admitted earlier, my hubris was my downfall. Did I have an inflated belief that I was not only marketable but also desirable and necessary? It is impossible to know for sure, even with the benefit of years of reflection, but I am certain that my expectations were out of synch with reality. After over two years with virtually no income, I finally decided that I had to do something, anything, to jump-start my stalled career. I made the difficult decision to change agents.

I called the only other person I knew I could count on: Babette. She understood my strengths and my weaknesses. We also had a close personal relationship. Keri and I were at her wedding. I was one of the first people to call her when her first son was born. She knew me, and she believed in me. Within a matter of weeks things began to change. Babette landed a series of short-term assignments that kept me afloat while we looked for a more permanent position. Our goal was to reinvent me.

In television terms, two years is a lifetime. I had been out of the spotlight too long to simply pick up where I had left off. I had to take one or two steps *backward* before I could again begin to move *forward*. Babette got me an interview with the syndicated news magazine *Inside Edition*. I flew to New York to meet the show's executive producer, and he was extremely gracious. His first question was, "You've anchored a national newscast for years. Why would you want to come to our show as a correspondent?" I was completely honest. I told him that I had to start over, and this was my opportunity to do just that. I got the job.

When I was at CNN, the O.J. Simpson trial gave me a unique opportunity to make my mark. Within months of joining *Inside Edition*, lightning struck again. The Michael Jackson molestation trial became a four-month national soap opera. Even though cameras were not allowed in the courtroom, the case captivated viewers. The witness list included a cast of characters who proved to be engaging and oddly entertaining.

Peter was the trial's media coordinator working as a liaison between the court and the television and radio networks and newspapers. Virtually every media outlet had one reporter there with a court-assigned pass, guaranteeing them a seat in the courtroom for the duration of the trial. Peter soon recognized that I was the only reporter there every day who was also a California lawyer, making me uniquely qualified to discuss the trial not only as a journalist, but also as an attorney. Peter single-handedly reinvigorated my career by putting me in front of the microphone outside the courtroom at each break in the trial. Within a matter of weeks, I became one of the de facto analysts for virtually every television and radio network. I provided all their programs with a brief legal synopsis of each day's events. I also became a regular nightly guest on CNN, FOX and MSNBC. By the end of the trial, I knew that from a professional standpoint, *I was back.*

A year later, I ran into Kenny at an event. Within days, he began courting me to return to him as a client. He bombarded me with calls, sometimes two or three a day. For months he wooed me, asking me to come back. This was not business, he said, "This is personal." I was flattered, perhaps too much so. Again, my ego was my undoing. Kenny's attention instilled in me an inflated sense of importance. Conceit clouded my judgment. I abruptly left Babette and returned to Kenny.

I had been so terribly disappointed in Kenny by our lack of results in the past that I mistakenly perceived that this was an opportunity to make things right. There was unfinished business between us. But I had done something horrible. I betrayed a friend. Babette had been eager to help me when I was desperate and I needed help. She believed in my abilities when I was consumed with self-doubt. She propped me up, emotionally and professionally. She was my advocate and my savior. I let her down. Twice.

Even after I left her, Babette remained gracious and supportive. We ran into one another on several occasions, and she always asked about Keri and our children, and she wanted to know how my career was going. Several months ago, I wrote her a letter expressing my remorse for having left her. I offered her an honest, heartfelt apology, without asking anything in return. I knew that I had wounded her in a deep, personal way. I needed to formally acknowledge and express my regret, remorse and sorrow for hurting her. She didn't deserve that from a client whom she had considered a friend as well.

I followed up my letter with a phone call. She was gentle and understanding and accepted my apology. I did not offer the apology in an effort to absolve myself of guilt or simply make myself feel better. That really isn't the purpose of an apology, anyway. It was solely for Babette—the person I had hurt. I could not take back my actions. But I felt relieved and satisfied that I had not let an opportunity pass to say something that we all too often fail to say. That apology ultimately led me back to Babette in a more meaningful way. She is my agent once again, and she has always been my friend.

Some wrongs simply can't be made right—at least not in the traditional sense, but an apology can go a long way. I honestly believe that it is never too late to apologize as long as it is genuine.

I am not talking about an insincere "sorry for being a horrible person all these years" but a real, honest offering of apology. Not to absolve you of guilt but to say to the other person—*YOUR* feelings matter to me, and I am sorry for hurting you.

Trite? Simple? Neither.

A true apology can do wonders for the soul. It has for mine.

UNDERSTANDING

"Everything that irritates us about others
can lead us to an understanding of ourselves."
—Carl Jung (1875-1961)

"The world only goes round by misunderstanding."
—Charles Baudelaire (1821-1867)

KERI AND I BECAME ENGAGED WHEN I WAS TWENTY-
FIVE, AND SHE WAS TWENTY-FOUR. We expected it to be one
of the most wonderful times in our lives. On the whole, it
was a magical period. But planning the wedding also created
a nightmare for us and drama within our families.

The fallout from the adoption and my later
reconciliation with my father still touched a raw nerve with
my mom and Gery. Inviting James to the wedding ignited
an all out war. My mom made it clear that if *he* were invited,
she would not attend. My father, meanwhile, felt wounded
by being excluded from the ceremony itself. I had invited my
father and his wife, my two brothers, my uncle and his wife
and two of his friends to attend as guests only. For a time, it
seemed as if we could appease everyone and simply move
forward and enjoy the event. Again, I was wrong.

Very early on the morning of my wedding I received a call from my father. He sounded extremely upset. After all the histrionics Keri and I had endured to get to this day, my father told me that he would *not* be coming to my wedding after all. He said he felt slighted because he was not involved in the procession and was not given a list of guests to invite. He claimed that my mother had controlled me, and he held *me* responsible for not standing up to her and defending him. I made it perfectly clear that he was not coming because he had a *right* to be there; he had given up that right a dozen years earlier when I was adopted. He was coming because I *wanted* him to be there. He was an *invited guest*. An important guest, but a guest, nonetheless.

I distinctly remember the nervous glances at the reception, searching in anticipation for the appearance of my father. True to his word, he never showed. The ceremony itself went off without a hitch. My best man, Josh, walked me down the aisle and into Keri's arms. It was a beautiful day, but marred, in part, by the absence of my father. The tension and anticipation tarnished what should have been a blissful event for my new bride. Little did we know that the real drama had only begun.

Keri and I spent part of our honeymoon in New York City, where my brother Christian was living. We visited Chick, and he informed us that my father's anger was so intense that my relationship with him was now over. There would be no more contact whatsoever.

Less than a dozen years after my adoption, I felt like I was left once again. Despite the estrangement, Chris and I remained close, and I also kept in contact with my younger brother, Anthony. My wedding seemed to accomplish what the adoption could not do—my father and I were now, officially, divorced.

Our second major reconciliation took several years to achieve. It was part serendipity and primarily a result of Keri's strength and determination. Keri was selling airtime at the local ABC television station in Los Angeles. She noticed that one of the scheduled guests for the daily local talk show *AM Los Angeles,* was none other than James Darren. He was there to promote his ABC television series, *TJ Hooker.*

Keri's shyness is often mistaken as weakness, but she has always shown a quiet strength of will and character. While she was still stinging from my father's rebuke, Keri set aside her own feelings and unbeknownst to me, decided that enough was enough—my father and I needed to see each other again. Keri waited outside the studio door and as my father left the set, she approached him, delivering a very simple message. She told him that he was missing out on a relationship with his oldest son, who still loved him very much. More importantly she said, "When we have children you will miss out on their lives as well. Don't wait until it is too late." Whatever she said clearly touched him. He invited us to dinner that night with Evy.

We often hear that time heals all wounds, and apparently our time apart was sufficient to mend our emotional injuries. It was uncomfortable at first, but within a few minutes, it was as if we had never been apart. It still surprises me that there was virtually no discussion whatsoever about the void in each of our lives or the rift that caused it. There was almost an unspoken agreement between us not to broach the subject at all. Perhaps the feelings were still too raw. Instead, we simply picked up where we had left off. He was my still father, and I was still his son. We were wounded, but we had survived—again.

Now, more than 25 years later, I understand so much more about the intense rage sparked by our wedding and the rift between my mother and father. Some fences apparently can't be repaired. My mother felt that he had relinquished all rights and interest in me. The adoption made that perfectly clear. The years of fighting should have been over. Why did *she* need to continue to suffer, and why should *his* feelings be considered at her expense? In her view, *he* had no right to attend the ceremony, not even as a guest. I understand. The irony, of course, is that *the adoption was never necessary for us to be a family. We already were.*

My father, on the other hand, had made it clear to me many times that his regret over his decision to allow the adoption did not negate his love for me or his desire to remain a part of my life. In retrospect, I believe that he could *never* have attended the wedding, no matter what his intentions. Showing up at such an event with my mom, along with my legal father Guy, may have been tantamount, in James' mind, to a public humiliation over his transgression. I believe it would simply be too painful for him to be viewed, and perhaps judged, for doing what he did, especially something that could never be undone. But there is nothing to judge. It is done. *We can either move forward, or we will be trapped in our own painful pasts.* To this day, my father believes that I was stolen from him. It is not necessary for me to *agree* with him, but I do acknowledge and *understand* his feelings.

Again, *I don't intend to take sides in a battle I cannot ever hope to win.* It is counterproductive and, frankly, far too painful. Plus, I always lose. Instead, I choose to focus on the positive. I am so fortunate to have a mom, a dad and a father. I am also so lucky to have Keri's parents, Horty and Artie, who have always embraced me and loved me as if I were their own son. I have a wealth of blessings in my life. Who am I to complain for having such a gift?

Isn't it time for you to show some understanding? Arguments often turn toxic and so can the sore feelings they evoke. Real understanding can be the salve to heal those wounds. It takes effort and requires setting your ego aside long enough to recognize that your own feelings are not the only ones involved. It requires selflessness, which ultimately gives you back so much more in return.

COMPASSION

"How far you go in life depends on your being tender
with the young, compassionate with the aged, sympathetic
with the striving, and tolerant of the weak and the strong—
because someday you will have been all of these."
—George Washington Carver (1864-1943)

COMPASSION IS FEELING SYMPATHY OR SORROW FOR
ANOTHER ALONG WITH A DESIRE TO RELIEVE THAT SUFFERING.
As a local and national broadcaster, I have met and
interviewed many people all across the country for which
many might conclude that all hope had ended. Some of
these individuals faced challenges that would outwardly
appear almost insurmountable. Yet a common thread
binding many of them was a spirit and determination to beat
the odds—to triumph over tragedy. I truly believe that all of
them lived better if not longer lives because of that attitude.

It is difficult to remain detached when covering
many stories. Some situations and people can touch you
deeply, despite your best efforts to remain objective. When
interviewing someone about a particularly sensitive subject,
I always try to treat him or her with respect and dignity. I
am always mindful that to them, this is not a story, this is

their life. One of the most meaningful lessons came following the verdict in the O.J. Simpson criminal trial.

FRED

I had been the chief anchor for CNN's gavel-to-gavel coverage of the lengthy trial, which had, for months, served as a national soap opera, galvanizing the population along racial lines. Having seen every bit of evidence in the case, there was no doubt in my mind that Simpson carried out the brutal double murders. I maintained my on-camera objectivity and never once gave my opinion during the trial, not even to my family. Given the poor manner in which the case was presented by the prosecution and the fact that the jury was sequestered for months, feeling like prisoners themselves, I was not surprised by the verdict. I also understood the political and psychological reasons behind the unanimous vote of not guilty.

Shortly after the verdict, I was filling in as host of *Larry King Live* and my main guest that night was Fred Goldman, the father of slain Ron Goldman. Seated next to Goldman was Dan Petrocelli, Goldman's attorney in the upcoming civil trial against Simpson. Goldman eventually won that case handily, even though no money has ever been collected on the $35 million plus verdict. At one point during the live interview, Fred's voice became shaky, and he began to cry. I know that most people view television reporters as heartless, but rather than allow the camera to remain on Fred as he started to break down in front of millions of viewers, I turned my attention and my next questions toward Dan Petrocelli. I knew that this respite would enable Fred to regain his composure. The interview was extremely difficult for Fred. It was just days after he watched the man he believed killed his son walk free to a hero's welcome.

When I got home following the broadcast, my phone rang. It was CNN's assignment desk calling to let me know that Fred Goldman asked if I would call him, which I did. Fred thanked me for showing him respect, kindness, and most of all compassion, during the interview. It was both a personal and professional highlight for me. I treated Fred the way I hoped that I would be treated. The lesson continues to make a tremendous difference in the way I try to live my life.

More than fourteen years after the murder of Ron Goldman and Nicole Brown Simpson, I still speak with the Goldman family. I have interviewed Fred and his daughter, Kim, many times since the trial. They know that I respect them and remain sensitive to their loss.

"Compassion is the basis of all morality."
—Arthur Schopenhauer (1788-1860)

BETH

Years later, the family member of another crime victim also touched me deeply. Natalee Holloway was on a high school graduation trip to Aruba when she suddenly went missing on the last morning of her vacation. Her case became an international story, in part, because this young, beautiful girl was alleged to have been killed by three local boys, one of them the son of a prominent judge. But the main reason this story remained in the headlines for months was because of a single force of nature named Beth Twitty, Natalee's mom.

I had met Beth for an interview in the Los Angeles bureau for *Inside Edition.* Something about Beth affected me immediately. She has a mom's tenderness and tenacity, and I could see that, despite her intense pain, she was not one to be crossed when it came to defending her child. Months later, I flew to Aruba to take her to dinner. It was her last night there before returning home to Birmingham, Alabama. It had been made clear to her by local authorities that she was no longer welcome on the island. I did not go there for an interview. I flew there to see first hand how she was coping with the fact that, months after her daughter's disappearance, she was no closer to finding answers. I spent the evening with Beth and two of her dear friends. We did not speak much at all about the case—she had done so virtually nonstop on every national morning show and cable news channel for weeks on end. I was especially happy that one of her friends told me that it was the first night in a long time that she had seen Beth smile. In many ways it was like a dinner with new friends, not at all like a reporter and subject.

Our connection was obvious. Beth and I each had a daughter who had just graduated from high school. Mine was off to a New York college, while hers never lived to attend her first semester. We both had sons named Matthew, hers was a bruiser of a football player for his high school team and mine was not yet eight years old. But they were each still our little boys. We were two parents talking about the unimaginable—the loss of a child.

Since that dinner, I flew to Beth's home on two different occasions to update her story, and she came to my home when she was in Los Angeles on her whirlwind media tour. My daughter, who was Natalee's age, had wanted to meet Beth, and I was reticent to introduce them, out of concern that it might upset Beth. She was gracious and cordial and seemed genuinely interested in my family and said she loved to keep in touch with her own daughter's friends. Our bond was forged by our similarities and the compassion we showed one another as parents and as people. I speak with her from time to time to see how she is doing because I genuinely care about her. I know that she will never find closure for her loss, but I am hopeful that she will find solace and happiness.

"If you want others to be happy, practice compassion. If you want to be happy, practice compassion."
—The Dalai Lama

GEORGE

In April 1998, George Michael was still a huge international pop star when he was arrested on a misdemeanor charge of lewd conduct. George allegedly exposed himself to an undercover cop in the men's room at a Beverly Hills park. It was a devastating blow to his fans and possibly to his career as well.

There was tremendous competition among the networks to land his first interview. NBC had promoted the interview, to be broadcast on the upcoming Sunday edition of *Dateline*, but our bookers at CNN were able to land the interview for me first, trumping NBC. We promised to air it Friday night around the world, which, given the time zone, would have been Saturday morning in his native England.

George agreed to a no-holds-barred interview. There were no ground rules whatsoever. We agreed to do the interview "live to tape" meaning it was to be recorded, but it would be played without editing at least once, in its entirety.

When George arrived, he looked like a nervous wreck. This was a man who routinely performed live before tens of thousands of screaming fans. But he was jumpy and appeared very uncomfortable. I spent an hour with him in the "green room" outside our studio, trying to calm him down. I made it very clear to him that this was not a prosecution, nor was it a persecution. It was to be a conversation—nothing more. I had no agenda. I planned to ask about the arrest, of course, but I was not there to embarrass him.

It was finally time for the interview. A camera recorded our walk from the green room into the studio. When we sat in our chairs, George seemed to have calmed down, but perhaps five minutes into the interview, I asked that the cameras be shut down. George had been stammering, and he looked so nervous that the interview was virtually unusable. I told him to take a deep breath and relax. This was not a trial. It was an interview. We took a short break, and then I said,

"Let's start again from the top." We did.

George finally gained his composure and within minutes, I was the one who would be stunned. He said on camera, "This is as good of a time as any. I want to say that I have no problem with people knowing that I'm in a relationship with a man right now. I have not been in a relationship with a woman for almost ten years."

He had just "come out" on international television!

About his arrest, he said, "The truth is I put myself in an extremely stupid and vulnerable position. I don't feel any shame. I feel stupid and reckless for having allowed my sexuality to be exposed in this way." The other shocking revelation: He said that the incident in the park was not his first time. He had done this before. He apologized to all his fans. It was a blockbuster interview that received international coverage.

After our interview it was clear that George felt an enormous weight had been removed from him. His mood lifted, and he smiled for the first time in the two hours since we met. I later learned that George was so adamant that our interview air Friday night in the US and Saturday morning in the UK because he feared the British tabloids were planning to "out" him as a homosexual in the Sunday papers. He wanted to make the announcement himself, on his own terms. It was a coup for my network and for me, but George seemed to feel it was a victory for himself as well.

Months later, I interviewed Elton John for a separate story. He and I hit it off right away, and he invited me to an event that night being held in his honor. I was in Cannes a few months later, covering the film festival, and I got a phone call at my hotel early one morning. It was Elton. He lived in nearby Nice, and he invited me to join him and his boyfriend that night for dinner at his home. During our meal, he told me how much he appreciated the interview I had done with his friend, George, a few months before. He said that George felt so relieved about doing the interview and, more importantly, about the respect and kindness I had shown him. Elton thanked me for being compassionate in my handling of such a sensitive and emotional topic.

It reaffirmed what I had always believed. Stories come and go. They don't matter nearly as much as the relationships you forge along the way. Trust is a precious commodity, and once squandered it is difficult to earn it back. I had treated George Michael the way I would like to be treated. Nothing more. Nothing less.

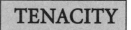

TENACITY

"Energy and persistence conquer all things."
—Benjamin Franklin (1706-1790)

"Knowing trees, I understand the meaning of patience.
Knowing grass, I can appreciate persistence."
—Unknown

I LEARNED PERSISTENCE FROM MY MOM. She grew up poor in South Philadelphia. The one extravagance she enjoyed was getting a new pair of shoes at the beginning of each school year. She was beautiful and intelligent, and she had an irrepressible drive. She knew early on that if she were to succeed, she had to leave her hometown and never, ever take "no" for an answer. The word simply didn't appear in her vocabulary.

She was only sixteen when I was born in Los Angeles. Her marriage to my father ended before she turned nineteen. I was my mom's partner in crime during those early years. I was her sole possessor of love and beauty and hope for a brighter future. She instilled in me so much love and empowered me to believe I could accomplish anything.

My mom worked as a fashion model by day and as a cashier by night in order to support us. Through sheer determination, she landed a sales job with the clothing manufacturer for whom she was modeling. She was now a woman succeeding in a man's world. Within a few years she was not only the company's top sales person, she had become the sales manager. When she made an offer to buy part of the company and was turned down, she reacted in the only way she knew how—she quit her stable, high-paying position and risked everything in order to start her own clothing company.

Over the years my mom battled several serious health issues. At twenty-six she endured the emotional and physical trauma of a hysterectomy. To have had this done at such a young age now sounds cruel and barbaric. Years later, when I was in college, my mom spent more than two months in the hospital being treated for a ruptured disc that rendered her nearly unable to walk. I was delivering pizzas at the time, and I would often schedule my last delivery of the night to Cedars-Sinai Medical Center. My mom and I shared some of my fondest memories over a special meatball sandwich made just for her.

Years later, her doctors surmised that a reaction to the anesthesia from one of her several surgeries caused her to develop the liver disease, primary biliary cirrhosis. For nearly twenty years she showed virtually no symptoms from the illness, which many people mistakenly believe is the result of alcohol consumption. That is ironic, given the fact that my mom never drank. She regarded the disease as yet another challenge, and she soon became involved with local and national charities providing seed grants for liver research and support for patients and their families. Before long, she was president of one of those charities.

Shortly after her sixty-fifth birthday, her liver began to fail, and she was quickly put on the list for a transplant. Her wait on the national registry was relatively short, just over six months, thanks in part to the fact that she had an unusual blood type. She faced the surgery like she faced all the challenges throughout her life, with grace and confidence. Was she frightened? Of course she was. But she was also courageous. She believed that she would recover—because that's the only outcome she would accept. The operation proved more problematic and difficult than we could have imagined. Within two days, her *new* liver was failing, and my mom, who because of her young age had been as much my peer as my parent throughout my life, was suddenly looking old and frail. I was terrified that I might lose her.

Amazingly, another donor liver was quickly found, and a second life-saving surgery was hastily scheduled. Before she was taken into surgery, my mom called for her children and grandchildren. Her strength was nearly drained, and the natural sparkle in her hazel eyes had dulled. I moved close to her and held her hand, and I was stunned when, with an unsteady hand, she wrote a single unforgettable word on a tablet. She wanted to say "goodbye" to those she loved the most. She did not expect to make it through the night. It was the only time I ever saw my mom defeated. I was terrified, but I refused to believe that this was the end.

The doctor who had performed both transplants came out of this latest surgery and, despite the recent complications, seemed confident and relieved that my mom would indeed make it after all. "She is a fighter," he said. It's something we knew all along. She had fought all her life — and that tenacity never let her down. Now, several years after her transplant, my mom is still fighting and enjoying her life.

"If at first you don't succeed, before you try again, stop to figure out what you did wrong."
—Leo Rosten (1908-1997)

Success cannot come without failure. More importantly, it is usually only *after* numerous failures that one finally achieves success. The key, of course, is not the failure itself, but what is *learned from it* and one's determination to *continue despite it.* That, of course is at the heart of tenacity. It is the refusal to give up or give in to failure and persevering despite all odds, often moving contrary to conventional wisdom.

In thinking about my mom's struggle to survive, I began to examine those things in my life that were worth fighting for. Then I began to wonder what I could accomplish if I continued to fight instead of just giving up?

How would your life be different if you replaced the words, "I can't" with an attitude of doggedness and determination? If, despite all odds and all disappointments, you continued to move forward until you finally achieved whatever it is you are after, just imagine how much richer *your* life could be. Now, consider how that tenacity would change even the last day of your life. It would be easy to sit and wait for the inevitable, but really living those final twenty-four hours might bring some of the greatest gifts imaginable. Without pushing forward you would never discover them.

MUSIC

"After silence, that which comes nearest
to expressing the inexpressible is music."
—Aldous Huxley (1894-1963)

"Music is the wine that fills the cup of silence."
—Robert Fripp

WHAT IS LIFE WITHOUT MUSIC? I cannot even imagine it. It is as important to me as oxygen.

For years, my home has been filled with guitars. They hang in almost every room—my bedroom, our children's rooms, in hallways, the living room, the den. I even have a home studio, with—guitars. Since the age of thirteen, they have been my instrument of choice.

When I was nineteen, my dream was to become a record producer and songwriter. I had played guitar daily for years and music was one of the most important aspects of my life. It is both an outlet of expression and a source of emotion and passion. I had yet to declare a major at UCLA, and I decided that music would be the field I would pursue. I had taken a number of music courses, which surprisingly, proved to be the most challenging classes I had taken in college. In order to be accepted into the School of Music, you had to pass an audition, which included being able to play two instruments and demonstrate the ability to sight-read a classical composition on the piano. I found a piano teacher and soon began taking lessons.

I routinely walked from class to class on the enormous campus with a cassette tape recorder in hand. At the time this was the vanguard of technology, having recently displaced eight- track tapes as state of the art. Whenever the muse struck, I was ready to record my ideas for lyrics and melodies. My piano teacher assisted me in setting those ideas onto paper, as I was still learning how to properly notate music.

I was most proud of one song in particular. It was, not surprisingly, a love song. My taste in music for playing guitar always tended toward hard rock, southern rock and jazz, but my writing and singing leant themselves to sappy love songs. When I became proficient in playing my song on the piano, I mustered up the courage to share it with my father. We had only reconciled a few years earlier, and I needed to share the song with him. Throughout his career as an actor he had also made his mark as a singer, both in records and performing for years in Las Vegas. While I was happy with my song, the true artistic test, for me, was to gain his approval.

I went to his home and, with some trepidation, I sat at the piano in his living room and began to play and sing my composition. I played sheepishly at first, but with each line my confidence and voice grew stronger. Then, quite surprisingly, one of the most memorable and validating moments in my life occurred. While I was playing the final verse, I felt my father's arms reach around me and hold on tightly. At first I could only hear, and then I turned to see, that he was crying. It was the only time in my life that I had seen my father cry. It touched me so deeply that I was able to move him with something I had written. More importantly, I felt it was a confirmation that even though we were no longer legally father and son, there was an inseparable bond between us. A legacy was passed from one generation to another that could not be erased by a court decree.

My father told me how proud he was, but frankly he didn't need to say a word. He arranged to record a rough version of the song, called a demo, and he hired a respected producer and several talented studio musicians, and we spent what I still regard as the best time in my life in a recording studio. My father was now singing the words and music that *I had written*. If talent had been passed from father to son, it was now the son giving back to the father, directing him in the studio.

I would not be in a studio again with my father for another twenty years. This time *I* was to be the one beaming with pride. While he had made his mark early on as a singer, my father's career eventually took him exclusively into acting and directing. For more than a decade he gave up singing altogether, almost to the point where he thought he would never perform professionally again. Then, he was cast in *Star Trek: Deep Space Nine* as a hologram of a '50s-style lounge singer. In each episode he would perform a Frank Sinatra classic and dispense advice to the lovelorn.

Those episodes led to a contract with a record company, and my father ultimately cut his first new album in nearly twenty years. It was recorded at the famed Capitol Records studio where Sinatra himself had immortalized some of his most famous tracks. Many of the musicians hired had, in fact, played on those very songs. At the time, I was anchoring *Showbiz Today* on CNN, and I was there with a crew, taping part of his recording session for an upcoming story. I remember having my nervousness quickly turn to pride as I saw him in his element.

Singing those songs was as effortless and natural for him as breathing. The music seemed to flow through him and revealed to me a talent I had always known was there, but never witnessed first hand. Again, we were bound together by music.

"To stop the flow of music would be like the stopping of time itself, incredible and inconceivable."
—Aaron Copland (1900-1990)

RICHARD

A friend who also shared my passion for guitars introduced me to Richard.

Richard and his wife Annetta owned a small business, which they ran out of their home in San Diego. They sold unique, handmade guitars and represented their builders, much like an art gallery represents artists. Richard had always recognized the intrinsic beauty in a fine handmade instrument. It was his dream to share that love with other musicians. I spoke with Richard over the phone, and I sought his guidance in choosing a new guitar. If you ask any guitarist how many instruments they need, the answer, invariably will be, "Just one more."

Richard's enthusiasm for guitars was contagious and what was initially intended to be a brief conversation, turned into several, hour-long discussions, followed by an invitation to his home. He told me that he would not sell me just any guitar and, he certainly could not let me buy one over the telephone without first holding it and playing it. He had to see if it "spoke to me." He said that this was not about money; it was all about putting the "right" guitar into a musician's hands. Richard was, in short, a matchmaker.

When we finally met in person, Richard was still recovering from a recent battle with cancer. He had been so weakened by the intense rounds of chemotherapy that he often found it difficult to get out of bed. But when I arrived at his home he was the perfect host. We spent an hour and a half looking at guitars. He displayed a childlike sense of joy when talking about the various instruments hanging on the walls in his living room and dining room. This was, after all, both his home and his showroom.

Richard showed distinct pride in discovering offbeat guitar builders throughout the country and championing their work. Many of the instruments were astronomically expensive, given the intricacy of the inlays and rarity of the woods and materials used. Each one was a treasure. But a great guitar, he told me, need *not* cost a fortune. He reached for one that he noticed had earlier caught my eye. It was a beautiful, gold-topped, art deco interpretation of a hollow-body electric guitar. He was so pleased when he realized he had just made another match.

We celebrated the discovery of my purchase by listening to music. He had put together a stereo system that would be the envy of any recording engineer, and he was so excited to watch my reaction at hearing music as if it was being played live in that very room. When I left, with my new guitar in hand, Annetta walked me to the door. She said that I had been one of his first visitors since going into remission and that, despite his fatigue, Richard seemed rejuvenated by the time we spent together. Richard had not just made a new customer that day; he had made a new friend.

I remember speaking with Richard several times after that first meeting. He always wanted to know how my "baby" was doing. I told him that I would play and cherish that guitar forever. I was happier still that we had met and found, in one another, someone to share our passions for guitars and music. I have always looked forward to Richard's e-mails, touting his latest discoveries, connecting with his clients and friends. The last e-mail I received was from his wife, Annetta, telling me that Richard lost his brave battle with cancer. Every note I play on that guitar will remind me of the musical gifts that defined Richard's life.

"Ah, music. A magic beyond all we do here!"
—J.K. Rowling

Music is magical, and it needn't cost a thing—singing a tune, listening to the radio, an album (remember vinyl records?) a CD, or an iPod. If I were to choose a soundtrack for the last day of my life—it would most definitely include the entire Beatles collection. Through their music, I have lived and experienced virtually every emotion in my life—from love to loss, happiness and solitude. I love rock, jazz, fusion, blues and country, but for me, the Beatles are timeless and perfect.

Here are some of my favorite life-defining albums (granted I am giving away my age here), which I would listen to on the last day of my life:

Beatles – "Abbey Road"
Deep Purple – "Machine Head"
Joni Mitchell – "Miles of Aisles"
Led Zeppelin – "II"
Eagles – "Hell Freezes Over"
Fleetwood Mac – "The Dance"
Jackson Browne – "The Pretender"
James Taylor – "One Man Band"

Music can create and even change your mood. It can remind you of a special moment or person in your life. It can emotionally take you to another place and time, without ever leaving your chair.

On my last day—I know what music will define the soundtrack of *my* life. Do you know what music would define *yours?*

LAUGHTER

"Laughter is the sun that drives
winter from the human face."
—Victor Hugo (1802-1885)

"The most wasted of all days is one without laughter."
—e.e. cummings (1894-1962)

I IMAGINE THAT I HAVE ONE DAY LEFT TO LIVE, AND
THEN I FOCUS ON LAUGHTER? You bet. There is nothing as
sweet as an infant's laugh, and I figure if we can enter this
world laughing, what better way is there to make our exit?

LARRY

Larry was a news cameraman. He did more than
videotape the world around him — he was an important *part*
of the world around him. He made a lasting impression on
everyone he met. He would always leave you laughing. I first
worked with Larry when I joined the local CBS television
station in Los Angeles. Shooting a story with Larry was never
work. The day would always be fun, and I would marvel at
his endless stories and sense of humor.

Larry was a prankster. It was widely rumored that in every hotel room Larry stayed on assignment, he would routinely take the artwork off the wall, remove the glass and sign the piece before placing it back in its frame. If you ever see a painting signed by L. Green, it might very well be his handiwork.

Every year Larry took it upon himself to edit the station's holiday gag reel that would include outtakes and bloopers from the year before, which would then be shown at the office wrap party. These videos were masterpieces, and everyone was fair game. It was a badge of honor to be included in Larry's annual "best of the worst." I recently found one of my most embarrassing moments posted on YouTube. I was anchoring the 6 a.m. newscast back in 1989. On one particular morning, when I sat in my chair, I realized that I had forgotten my earpiece, which was my electronic link to the director in the control room above the studio. I was alone on the stage, and I decided to run to my desk two buildings away and retrieve it. I miscalculated the time, and when I returned to the set, I could hear the director over the loudspeaker counting down, ten seconds to air. By the time we went live, I was so out of breath, and it appeared that I was either crying or having a heart attack on the air. It was January 2nd, so some viewers might have simply presumed I was badly hungover from the night before. I hadn't seen that tape in more than fifteen years, and I laughed, realizing that it was Larry who had saved it from the trash bin.

Larry played electric guitar, and he especially loved to play the blues. One year he organized a band at the station, which I decided to name "Bad News." It seemed appropriate. Larry enlisted the station's main anchor, Jim

Lampley, the 11 o'clock Executive Producer, the Managing Editor and yours truly to practice once a week at a nearby rehearsal hall. We were missing a bass player, and somehow, Larry convinced someone who did not even work at the station to join our band. I knew him only by the name "Fly." For one night, the members of "Bad News" were rock stars. We performed in front of hundreds of people at our Christmas Party, which that year was held at the famous Hollywood venue, The Palladium. It was a dream come true—even if we did not sound nearly as good to the partygoers as we did to ourselves.

Years later, long after I left the station, Larry continued to reach out to me as he did to all his friends, making each of us feel as if we were the most important friend he had. It was his unique and endearing quality. He was a boy in a man's body who just wanted to hang out and play. When I took up motorcycling in my forties, I ran into Larry at a local hangout where weekend warriors often met on Sunday mornings. There he was on his motorcycle. He laughed when he saw me pull up on mine. Both our bikes were Harleys, and each of us was clinging to our teenage fantasies for as long as possible.

The last time I spoke with Larry, he called and told me he was heading to the Persian Gulf to shoot a story for the one-year anniversary of 9/11. He said that when he returned in a few weeks time we would meet up for another ride. We never took that ride. Larry was taping from a military helicopter when the pilot accidentally clipped the mast of a ship. The collision forced the chopper to make a crash landing. Larry was the only one onboard not belted in, because of the way in which he had to lean out of the chopper to film. He was ejected from the open doorway and killed instantly.

Larry's funeral, just like his life, was a major event. So many people attended, that it was held outside on the back lot of CBS studios. A huge Jumbo-Tron monitor was erected, similar to the ones used at outdoor stadiums, to enable all his friends and family to see the many mourners who were there to speak about Larry and to show some of the many videos he had shot and edited. It was a moving tribute, filled with tears and laughter, just the way he would have wanted it. Larry never had a chance to say goodbye, but he was always the first to say hello and make you laugh. I still smile whenever I think of him.

ADVENTURE

"Life is either a daring adventure or nothing."
—Helen Keller (1880-1968)

FLYING, DRIVING AND VAMPIRE HUNTING

While I do not generally consider myself to be an adventurous person, I have never shied away from trying something new. My dad, Gery, owned and piloted his own private plane. I took my first lesson when I was only eight years old. The reasoning behind it, however, is not as cavalier as it sounds. My dad simply wanted to make sure that whenever I was with him in the plane, I would be able to land safely in the event anything happened to him while we were flying.

While I never actively pursued flying as a hobby, being in the air, at the controls of a light plane, is an extraordinary experience. It is liberating and exhilarating, peaceful and demanding—soaring ten thousand feet over the ground, being simultaneously relaxed and fully alert.

In 1998, while I was an anchor at CNN, I was invited to participate in the Toyota Pro-Celebrity Race. The event precedes the annual Grand Prix event in Long Beach,

California, and pits a field of twenty celebrities against each other. While many of the guests were, in fact stars, including Queen Latifah, Cameron Diaz, Jim Belushi and Catherine Bell, my involvement somehow devalued the celebrity aspect of the race. I was honored just to be there.

We each drove a specially modified Toyota Celica for ten laps around the same course that the Formula drivers were to use for the main event. For two months before the race, we spent several weekends of intensive classroom and in-car training at the famed Willow Springs track, just north of Los Angeles. We learned how to drive competitively from some of the best instructors around. At first, they rode along with us in the cars, and eventually, we were cut loose to drive solo and compete against each other in time trials. It only took one near-fatal moment for us all to realize that it might not be such a good idea to put a group of relatively untrained drivers behind the wheel of high-performance cars on a racetrack.

I had a crew from CNN follow me one training day for a behind-the-scenes story we were planning on the celebrity race. If there was one wild card in our group, it was Belushi. His bravado could easily be mistaken for recklessness, but I suspect much of what he did was for the inevitable reaction that would follow. He certainly got a strong reaction from my crew. On his final practice lap, going well over one hundred miles an hour on the straightaway, he came within inches of taking out my cameraman. We all caught our breath and laughed it off, but my adrenaline was pumping for more than an hour. Even before the race itself, the adventure had begun.

For someone like me, who grew up watching the Indy 500 and wishing that I could be one of those guys behind the wheel, it was a fantasy come true. Race day proved to be especially challenging because for the first time in the event's history, it was raining. There was concern that, given our lack of experience, there could be trouble. While several of us, including me, did, in fact, spin out on the track, amazingly, there were no collisions and no injuries. Belushi didn't participate that day, so I can only imagine what would have happened with him driving the course. In fairness, he was a better driver than most of us. I was content to finish sixth, but it did sting a bit knowing that Cameron Diaz beat me handily.

> **"You must pray that the way be long, full of adventures and experiences."**
> —Constantine Peter Cavafy (1863-1933)

I think the most adventurous thing I ever did involved saying "yes" to a casual last minute invitation. I was at dinner with my friend, Eyton, who was producing a television series called *The World Scariest Places*. He was about to shoot an episode in Transylvania at Dracula's castle (no kidding—it's a real castle in Romania). I told him that his trip sounded amazing, and he said, perhaps not believing I would accept, "Why don't you come?" I looked at my wife, and she said, "Why don't you? You'd love it!" I took the cue and said yes before any of us could change our minds.

Within a few days I was on a plane (actually a few planes followed by a four-hour car ride). I was officially off on one of the true adventures of my life. It still strikes me as odd that many people have since asked me why in the world I chose to go. My response has always been, "Why wouldn't I?" I still haven't met anyone else who's been there.

It was everything I could have *ever* imagined and much I could *never* have imagined. After landing in Romania, a car drove me nearly five hours to our final destination—Timisoara, on the western edge of the country. With each kilometer, it seemed as if we were going back another year in time. The landscape was rural and familiar, resembling a storybook version of medieval times. Instead of cars, people rode on horse-drawn carts. If you can recall the famous scene in *The Wolfman* where Lon Chaney Jr. stumbles upon the old gypsy woman riding on a wagon filled with hay—I would swear I saw her on that trip. Many of the cottages between the expansive fields of green and grain looked like thatched huts that had probably been there for hundreds of years. Nearly every home had a rustic wooden fence and many yards had chickens running wild. The countryside was simple and so were the people, not yet tainted by the modern technologies, which have both seduced and trapped our generation. There was no traffic noise, no horns honking, no sound of air conditioners, just windows left open to catch the occasional breeze. Living in a major city as long as I had, the sound of birds and nature seemed oddly unfamiliar but welcome.

As we drew closer to the village where the castle was located, I saw the brief but harsh attempts by the former Soviet Union to modernize the area. Water and sewage pipes ran aboveground, marring the simple beauty of the modest stone streets. But otherwise, little had changed here since the 1500s. The inn I stayed at with my friend was centuries old. It was clear that electricity and plumbing were afterthoughts, installed years after the cozy rooms were first built. The windows did not even have screens, and, in a vain attempt to keep bugs out at night, we kept the windows open and curtains drawn as a makeshift barrier. The television shoot required us to work late into the night, and when we returned to our cottage, even at two in the morning, the innkeeper had a multi-course meal of local cuisine prepared for us. During one such meal, we were served what was ostensibly chicken, but it was so petite and there were so many unusual bones that I joked with my colleagues that we were probably eating bat.

The castle—Dracula's Castle—was austere and frightening, even in daylight. Its most famous resident, Vlad Tepes, was also known as "Vlad the The Impaler," and in more modern times as Count Dracula. In truth, he was actually not a Count at all. He was the much feared and ruthless Prince of Wallachia in the mid 1400s. His penchant for impaling people went far beyond his desire to terrify invading armies. He actually considered the deadly torture method to be a form of entertainment. It is estimated that as many as 30,000 people were killed in or around his castle. The interior courtyard was built with a distinct slope so that blood would flow out the front gates to frighten off intruders. Some of the rooms deep within the castle, which had been built specifically for torture, still suggested the distinct chill of death, all these centuries later. It was not a luxurious vacation, but it was an unforgettable experience. Had I said no to that invitation, I know that I would have always regretted the decision.

I did something that I never could have imagined doing. It still makes me smile to think that I was in that dank, centuries-old castle in the middle of the night, scared out of my wits and afraid to venture around alone. It was creepy, surreal and utterly fantastic. When I think back on that trip, it was really the spirit of adventure that got me there, not the plane.

Granted, my scenario provides only twenty-four hours to do something adventurous. In that short time frame, some things are logistically out of the question. It's impossible to scale Everest. Skydiving or bungee jumping, either of which could arguably hasten your exit, is each a valid consideration for a last great adventure. But I submit that the real adventure is borne *within*—it is the *spirit*, rather than the *action* that defines an adventurous soul. What adventures are left for you to experience? Have you said no only to later regret your decision? I suggest that you will more likely regret turning down an adventure than you will if you live one.

What have you always wanted to try but thought, "Maybe someday." I have come to the conclusion that—*today is that day*. I have embraced the idea of being open to adventure. I often like to take action without notice or planning. Embrace every experience and allow it to nourish you.

PASSION

"The happiness of a man in this life does not consist
in the absence but in the mastery of his passions."
—Alfred Lord Tennyson (1809-1892)

"Only passions, great passions,
can elevate the soul to great things."
—Denis Diderot (1713-1784)

MY MOM AND DAD USED TO TELL ME THAT WHEN
CHOOSING MY CAREER, I SHOULD FOLLOW MY PASSION. "Do
what you love, and the money will follow," Gery would say.
Sadly, I did not heed his advice right away. In college, I had
dreamed of becoming a songwriter and record producer. But
I was afraid; afraid of failing, I suppose. I decided to play it
safe. It is one of the true regrets of my life.

When I told my folks that I had made up my mind
to go to law school after college, they were shocked, as the
idea seemed to come out of the blue. It did. I thought that
by doing so, I would always have a marketable skill to fall
back on. But I missed the point. There is a reason why young
people take risks—they have few responsibilities, and,
therefore, they have little to lose.

Tabling my dreams almost killed them. During law school and for several years afterward, I never picked up my guitar. It sat in its case, tucked away in a closet. Then, one day, I felt it calling me back. I had bought that particular guitar when I was fifteen, and I spent several hours every day practicing and playing. The thought that I had almost abandoned it entirely now seems unbelievable to me.

Opening the guitar case again for the first time in years proved a revelation. It reignited a longing that I had suppressed almost to the point of extinction. I began to take lessons again in my thirties, and I tapped into a feeling that was as basic as breathing. I had rediscovered my passion. I vowed never to ignore it again. I continue to play nearly every day, even if only for a few minutes at a time — not just because I *want* to but because I *need* to. It replenishes my soul.

After my family, music is the most important thing in my life. It is a passion that I have happily shared with my children. Amanda began playing guitar at age ten. I bought her a 3/4-sized instrument to suit her smaller hands, and she began taking lessons. Within a few years she also began playing the electric bass. We share a love for much of the same music, and she actually keeps me feeling young by introducing me to new groups. A decade later, Matthew also gravitated to the guitar — both electric and acoustic. The music he loves also happens to be the same music I played when growing up. He became enamored of those same songs thanks in large part to the video games, *Guitar Hero* and *Rock Band,* which rely on "classic" rock. Through my kids, I am not only passing on my love and passion for music, but through those songs we form a unique and lasting connection to each other.

The guitars on display in my home serve two functions: they are visually beautiful and act as artwork on the walls. I have also found that when an instrument is out (as opposed to sitting in a case in the closet) you tend to play it more often. Each guitar has a distinct look, feel and sound. In their own way, each is a showpiece, but none are treated like museum pieces. They are meant to be touched, strummed, played and enjoyed. I almost imagine they are happiest when they are played. They are beautiful tools intended to make beautiful music. I cannot imagine a day of my life spent without making and listening to music.

Fortunately, I finally did follow another passion, which led to my career as a broadcaster. I love to talk. I always have. In elementary school, my parents were often called in for conferences with the teacher because I tended to talk during class. Much to my instructor's chagrin, when I was asked to repeat what she had just said, I was able to do so almost verbatim, even though I was talking to another student when she admonished me. It is a talent that served me well as an anchor and reporter, as I often wear an earpiece when I am live on the air. A producer often talks in my ear while I am reporting on camera. Talking and listening at the same time—I seemed to find the only job that rewards it. Not long after we got married, Keri joked that I was the only person she knew who could have a conversation with a bag of pretzels, so it seems natural that I would choose a career that enabled me to make a living just for talking.

Keri has a passion for plants and for flowers. She has followed that passion into her work, as she now assists a landscape designer. Like me with my guitars, she chooses to surround herself with the things that inspire her most. Look

out any window of our home, and all you will see is green—
even from the second-story rooms. We are no more than 100
yards from what's known as the "Wilshire Corridor," running
through one of the busiest areas in Los Angeles, yet we are
nestled in a horticultural cocoon. It is our peaceful, secret
garden. Inside our home, the rooms are adorned with flowers
cut from the plants that surround our house. They fill each
room with the fragrance of the outdoors.

What passions nourish your soul? What in your life
sustains you in a spiritual way? Identify that one thing you
cannot imagine living without. It is so easy to "grow up" and
take on the daily responsibilities of making a living that we
often neglect and enjoy the act of living our lives to the
fullest. I try to keep my own passions alive while also
encouraging my family to notice and nurture their own
passions. Ultimately, that enriches us all.

POSSESSIONS

"Riches do not delight us so much with
their possession, as torment us with their loss."
—Dick Gregory

"There must be more to life than having everything."
—Maurice Sendak

IT'S EASY TO GET CAUGHT UP IN THE CHASE FOR MORE AND MORE POSSESSIONS. Jewelry, cars, and other status symbols can be intoxicating. Isn't it curious how the more you get, the more you want? Sometimes too much can literally devalue the currency altogether and make each individual item somehow less precious.

When I was a teenager and had only one guitar, it somehow seemed more precious to me than when I owned fifty. I still have the electric guitar I got when I was fifteen, and it means more to me than you can imagine. Still, I admit, I have been victim to the seemingly unquenchable desire for more at various times throughout my life. We are told from the earliest age that *more is better*. We are bombarded with ads convincing us that we need a litany of products in order to truly be happy in life. We soon begin to define ourselves by *what we have*, rather than *who we are*. I suspect, when you finally begin to examine your own life, it will not focus on a list of all the things you bought in life but what you have brought to your life.

DANNY

Several years ago, I was introduced to a hero of mine. Danny is a master luthier, a guitar designer and builder, who created and handcrafted some of the most outlandish and beautiful guitars I had ever seen. While he is not well known to the general public, his instruments, among professional musicians, are both coveted and revered for their expression of whimsy, clarity and musicality. Here was a man who could have made millions of dollars mass-producing his designs, but he chose a dramatically different and far simpler path. Amanda and I spent a memorable afternoon with Danny, watching him work in his modest workshop and then sharing a peaceful lunch and revealing conversation. The experience shook both of our perceptions of success and happiness to the core.

Danny admitted to us he maintained no bank account. He lived in the same unassuming apartment for years and drove a ten-year-old car in a town where your identity is transmitted as much through what you drive as by what you do for a living. He didn't have health insurance or even know his own social security number. His production schedule was dictated by a basic rule: when he needed to make money, he built an instrument. He chose his clientele as carefully as he chose the wood for his guitars.

Despite his enormous and unique talents, one might think he would be envious of the financial success of the numerous rock stars for whom he built guitars. But this man had something I have rarely, if ever, seen up close. He was truly content and happy with his life. It was a life he lived *on his terms.* Danny said he had everything he *needed* and everything he *wanted.* Possessions were of no value to him as they did not really bring him happiness. Now years later, Amanda and I still speak about that day with a sense of longing and awe and perhaps a bit of envy. That dear, sweet guitar maker may have few material possessions, but in many ways he may be the richest man I have ever met.

It is not too late to try to determine *who you are,* not by examining what you own, but by identifying your *values,* your *likes,* your *dislikes.* Don't measure your own success by the perception of others. You will always fall short. In my current crisis I have often thought of the lessons that Danny taught me on that afternoon. I had failed to truly learn them until recently. I had been defining myself through what I had, and what I stood to lose, namely my house. I allowed that to make me feel diminished as a person. It consumed my life, and I almost allowed it to claim my life. It was nearly a fatal error.

"You can't take it with you."
—George Kaufman (1889-1961) & Moss Hart (1904-1961)

When I thought of having only twenty-four hours to live, when I was faced with the last day of my life, I realized, with more clarity than ever before, that we enter this world alone, and that's how we leave it. Through the prism of your last day what *really* looks most important to you? Think about what you *want* to be happy and what you really *need*.

I did. I discovered that what I needed most could never be bought or sold. But it still had to be earned and cherished.

SURPRISE

"One's life is not as fixed as one believes.
Surprises may lie in store for you; the unexpected often
tends to happen, sometimes bringing in its train the
most delightful change in one's life or circumstances."
—Elizabeth Aston

ERROL

YOU NEVER KNOW WHAT WONDERFUL SURPRISES LAY
JUST AROUND THE CORNER.

With the advent of the Internet, my hobby of guitar collecting escalated into a near obsession. I checked the daily stock of stores around the country, and I started buying and selling on eBay, trading one instrument for another, constantly looking for "the" guitar that in my heart I knew was more an ideal than a reality.

As often happened, one day I received a guitar that I knew immediately was not for me, so I listed it for sale again on eBay. It sold quickly. The buyer, Errol, lived in New York. He had amassed a huge number of positive feedbacks, letting me know he had a great deal of experience on eBay and that he had an impeccable record on the site, both as a buyer and seller. He wired the money into my account, and I promptly packed and sent him the guitar. I had purchased that particular instrument brand-new, directly from Gibson. I was the first person to open the box, so I advertised with confidence that it was in mint condition.

Almost immediately upon receipt, Errol e-mailed me and complained that the finish was not acceptable. He said that it had an "orange peel" appearance to it. I knew I could resell the instrument easily, so I immediately and without question wired him a full refund, plus an additional amount for return shipping. I asked if he would be kind enough to ship it back the following day. Errol was stunned—here I had entrusted him, a total stranger, with both my guitar and his money. He knew I was either an idiot or a really good guy, or maybe a bit of both.

My single action prompted him to e-mail me, and we began a cyber–pen pal relationship. We soon discovered that we were nearly the same age, had similar backgrounds and also shared a lifelong passion for music and guitars. It was the beginning of a beautiful friendship. Our e-mails soon evolved into telephone conversations.

Errol was a banker by trade, but he had built an elaborate professional home recording studio and was an incredibly talented guitarist and songwriter. He had recorded and distributed two full albums of material. Soon, we were talking nearly every day. Its familiarity and intensity reminded me of a grade-school friendship.

Errol told me he was planning a trip to Los Angeles, and I invited him to my home to meet my family and have drinks, before taking him out to dinner. I remember my wife's mom, Horty, asking me, half-jokingly, whether I could be sure this stranger I had invited over wasn't really a serial killer. We laughed, of course, but I also admitted that I couldn't really be certain. At the time, I had an open-air electric car made by Ford called the "Think." It was a two-passenger vehicle that was really more a novelty than a car, but it was licensed and street legal and reached a maximum speed of 25 miles an hour. My brief excursions were relegated to side streets and neighborhoods. Errol was staying at a hotel less than two miles away, and I told him I would pick him up and to look for the guy in the electric car. When he saw me, and noticed the stares and chuckles from the valets outside the hotel, it was *his* turn to wonder what he really knew about this lunatic from California, arriving in a glorified golf cart.

My friendship with Errol has grown far beyond our shared love of music. He is a confidant and advisor, and he is almost like another brother to me. Who would have believed that I could develop such an incredible life-changing relationship through as unlikely a place as eBay. I didn't even have to pay a commission!

We still talk nearly every day, and my family has visited Errol and his wife, Deb, in New York, and they have come to our home in Los Angeles. Both of my daughters have gone to school in New York, and I felt so relieved to know Errol and Deb were there as guardian angels to watch over them. Recently, Errol became our first houseguest ever in my twenty-six years of marriage. I told him about my friendships with Steve and Josh and warned him, that if I ever called him my "best friend," he likely had less than ten years left to live.

It really underscores the point, even on the last day of your life, who knows what incredible surprises await you? Even in those final hours, just imagine the possibilities. Every day offers that same potential of surprise, right up until that very last minute. Embrace it.

WONDER

"I hear babies crying. I watch them grow,
They'll learn much more than I'll never know,
And I think to myself, what a wonderful world"
—George David Weiss & Bob Thiele (1922-1996)

EXPECT THE UNEXPECTED. You didn't really think when you first opened this book that you'd be asked to imagine having only one day left to live, did you? But here you are, still with me on this journey. You have dealt well with surprise. Now it's time to share the experience of wonderment and joy.

LESSONS FROM PRESCHOOL

My daughter, Carly, finished her first year of college in New York and then returned home for the summer. When looking for a summer job, her first inclination was to work as an assistant at the very preschool she had attended as a toddler. I suspect that those children actually taught Carly lessons more valuable than she was able to teach them.

Carly is a natural caregiver. She is loving and nurturing, warm and inviting. Within a day, several of the children gravitated toward her and sat on her lap during story time, telling her that they loved her. Carly was soon coming home beaming about the silly things these kids had said or done. Her stories made all of us smile.

From an adult perspective, nothing in particular had happened, but through those little eyes, each day was new and extraordinary. Carly soon recognized the sense of wonderment and surprise these children were experiencing through the simplest of activities — petting a bunny, finger painting a keepsake to be displayed that night on the refrigerator door, making mud with sand and water.

Carly told me about a recent day when all the toddlers in her group were fascinated by Samson, the school's tortoise and unofficial mascot. Samson was eating a piece of lettuce and that single natural act utterly fascinated the children. One by one they began shouting, "Samson is eating! Samson is eating!" The fact that something so simple could become a source of pleasure and excitement should not be quickly dismissed.

Witnessing these precious children has enabled Carly to relive those basic and priceless joys offered by the tiny corner of the world of that preschool, just as she had enjoyed them when she was a small child. Samson was there when Carly was a child, and she probably had experienced, and long since forgotten, feeling the same excitement over watching Samson enjoying a meal. Listening to her describe the reactions of those little boys and girls, it was impossible not to be pleasantly reminded of my own youth, enabling me to recapture some of that lost innocence, if only for a moment.

Children are born with a sense of wonderment and easily find pleasure in the simplest of things—many of which we later either ignore, or choose not to appreciate any longer. Open your eyes—notice and then soak in the natural surprises all around you—a beautiful, sunny sky and a cool breeze, a child's smile. What at first blush appears mundane can really be magical. Allow yourself to experience it. I had almost forgotten that the most profound pleasures of all are the simplest ones.

Think about it—with only 24 hours remaining, isn't a sunrise breathtaking? Listen to the birds singing outside your window as dawn turns to morning. Feel the refreshing coolness of a lawn kissed by morning dew. How long has it been since you really appreciated, let alone noticed, the most basic of pleasures? If you ever lose the feeling, sit down for a few minutes with a child. What they can teach you is priceless.

PURPOSE

"The purpose of life is to live it, to taste experience
to the utmost, to reach out eagerly and without fear
for newer and richer experience."
—Eleanor Roosevelt (1884-1962)

MOVE WITH DIRECTION OR LOSE YOUR DIRECTION.

For years my daily routine was the same. Every
morning, after saying out loud my list of everything for which
I am grateful, I recited a list of words that helped me face
each day with purpose and positive energy. For too long I got
in the habit of just going through the motions of daily life
without a true sense of purpose.

It's easy to get off track. Long-term goals are realized
slowly, one day at a time. Life is like a map—it's important
to identify your destination and start planning your route.
Without a plan you don't know where you will end up, but
it will most likely NOT be where you really wanted to go.
That's what eventually happened to me. I think that's how I
ultimately got so far off course.

When you drive, you need fuel for your car. I have a
list of words that are like fuel for my soul—enabling me to

make the most of my journey every day. My personal mantra is a list I call the "Ten C's". I am committed to reciting this list out loud every morning before I am off to face the challenges of each day. It inspires me and helps me to meet those challenges in a positive way.

Here is my "power" list:

Calm
Cool
Connected
Compassionate
Charming
Creative
Comical
Curious
Confident
Centered

I always end on *"centered."* I then take a deep breath, hold it and then slowly release, letting go of tension and apprehension. I find it clears my head and gets me ready to face the day with strength and determination. These are words that work for *me*—you can find your own list that touches and motivates and inspires *you*. I like words that start with the same letter, there's a Zen-like feel that just seems right.

"The only true happiness comes from
squandering ourselves for a purpose."
—William Cowper (1731-1800)

PLAN IN ACTION

Those words inspire me. And they really work. I first
began using my list of "power" words shortly after I was hired
at CNN in 1990. That list—positive and strong, inspired me
to take *action*. The short-lived national entertainment show
I had been co-anchoring for Fox television was cancelled,
and I soon signed with CNN for only one year as Senior
Entertainment Correspondent. I was based in Los Angeles
and handled celebrity interviews, covered premieres and
awards shows and general entertainment news (far different
from the ubiquitous Hollywood tabloid-style coverage we see
today). I did not know if CNN would be the right fit for me,
and vice versa, which is why I prevailed on the network
executives to agree to only a one-year deal.

Around ten months into my contract, and at my own
expense, I scheduled a trip to the network's headquarters in
Atlanta, Georgia. I set up meetings with the president and
several senior Vice Presidents, none of whom I had ever met
in person. I boarded a red-eye flight from Los Angeles to
Atlanta and booked a room in the Omni Hotel, which was
located in the same complex as CNN. I had several meetings
set up back to back, enabling me to return home that night.
I went armed with various ideas for programming and
specials. I checked in at six in the morning, took a brief nap,

showered and changed into a suit and headed off for a day that I hoped might change my career.

During my first meeting, the executive asked what I was doing while I was in town. I told him that the purpose of my trip was solely to meet with him and the other bosses at the network. I told him that I was coming toward the end of my contract, and the purpose of my trip was not to say "goodbye," but rather to say "hello." I wanted the opportunity to establish a personal relationship so that when we spoke in the future we would have a better sense of one another. I shared with him several of my thoughts about the show and our coverage.

He was so stunned and impressed with my confidence and unorthodox approach that he said to me, "CNN may be cheap, but we're not that cheap. We are reimbursing you for your airfare and your hotel." Within two months I was named co-anchor of CNN's entertainment program, *Showbiz Today,* which I hosted for the next eight years. Did my positive attitude, my focus and my sense of purpose result in my promotion? I certainly believe that it did.

It was also on that trip that I first met the network's chairman, Tom, who later had such a profound and positive impact on my life. Again, I think there are no accidents. Purpose leads to action. For a time, I lost my sense of purpose. Thank goodness I rediscovered it in time.

LEGACY

"Person to person, moment to moment,
as we love, we change the world."
—Samahria Lyte Kaufman

WE ENTER THE WORLD ALONE. Ultimately, that is
how we will leave it. Along this journey our lives are
inextricably woven together. Touch one person, and you
indirectly touch all people. That is the mark you leave
behind.

My legacy is my children. If I achieve nothing else
in my lifetime, I have done all that I consider important
through the time spent and love given toward nurturing,
raising and guiding them. Amanda, Carly and Matthew are
the culmination of my life's work, hopes and dreams. I often
think back to the words of my old boss, Tom, at CNN: that
at the end of my life, my character will be measured by the
kind of person, friend, son, husband and father I have been.
I cannot imagine what my children might achieve, but I take
pride in knowing I will remain with them in spirit long after
I am gone. I have worked and sacrificed to give them the best
education available. I have sought to instill in them the

confidence to succeed in life, not just in their careers. That is my gift, my legacy.

AMANDA

She was our first-born, and she was the first grandchild in our family. The moment she came into the world, *our* world changed forever. She has been a blessing ever since. Every parent will tell you that his or her child is the most beautiful child in the world. I am no exception, except Amanda *was* the most beautiful baby I had ever seen. She soon made it clear that she was her own person. She never learned to crawl. Instead, she would scoot while lying on her back, actually wearing out a patch of fine baby hair on the back of her head. I used to joke that it resembled classic male pattern baldness. One day at around fourteen months old, she abruptly stood and began walking. From then on, she never looked back.

She was a tomboy, through and through. For a time as a child, she seemed to want to be a boy. In fact, her sister, Carly, almost three years younger, actually thought Amanda *was* a boy when she was still a toddler. Keri and I decided that as long as Amanda was a happy child, she should be allowed to be her own person. Water seeks it own level, no matter how hard you may struggle to fight it. I remember coming back from a business trip and almost falling over when I saw Amanda in a dress for the very first time. She was in the seventh grade, and she was stunning. In the course of that trip, I left behind a "son" and returned to find a young woman.

When she was twelve, Amanda became interested in moviemaking. She saved her money and bought a video camera and shot her first original short film. It was called *Director's Cut*, and it focused on a movie director who fell in love with the leading lady in a murder mystery he was filming, only to be stabbed to death by her in real life. Amanda enlisted my father to star in her first production. In the last shot, as the director is on the floor, bleeding and releasing his final breath, you hear a swell of music—the Dean Martin song "That's Amore." When I asked Amanda about this odd movie which she felt compelled to write and shoot, she said simply, "It's a love story, dad."

Amanda's quirkiness has always been her charm. She is studious and serious, sometimes to a fault. By age fifteen, she had already read two volumes of Proust. I was so touched when she chose to study both Art History and Communication at USC, degrees Keri and I had individually earned when we were in college. Amanda is the most sensitive and loving child a parent could ask for.

CARLY

Our second daughter's name was inspired by Carly Simon. Her life has been just as lyrical as Simon's music. Carly has always been a wonder to me. She glides through life, seemingly without effort and without a care. She is loving and gentle. Without saying a word, she can electrify a room simply by entering it. Her energy changed our household almost overnight. When she was a toddler, and I would tuck her in, she would ask me the same simple, profound question, night after night, "Do you wish you were me?" My answer to her was always the same, "Yes. I would love to be you even if just for a day." What must it be like to be so happy?

Carly and Amanda are best friends. They are opposites that attract and complement each other so completely. Like her sister, Carly showed an artistic side early on, but her talent was expressed through painting, drawing and photography. I suspect that Carly will satisfy her love for painting by becoming a makeup artist, a dream she has expressed since childhood. While it has been so rewarding to watch her become a beautiful young woman, it is also a bit difficult to see my little girl grow up.

MATTHEW

Matthew is our miracle boy. He is eleven years younger than Amanda and almost eight years Carly's junior. Not surprisingly, every member of his family has pampered him. In some ways he is the perfect blend of both of his sisters. He is quirky but funny, silly and serious, tough but gentle and always loving and loved. Through Matthew, I was able to relive my own early boyhood in ways that surprised me. He took the damaged parts and made them whole. I offer him love without condition.

Like both of his sisters, Matthew is a gifted artist. He showed a natural love of drawing as a young child. Early on, his work showed a clear understanding of depth and perspective that was innate and utterly sophisticated. Thanks to being around two older and supportive siblings, Matthew developed confidence early in life. He is disarmingly charismatic, and he has an odd and infectious sense of humor. His smile will take him far in life.

As the youngest child he gets spoiled more than we should allow, but I have no regrets and no remorse when it comes to any of my children. They are amazing, wonderful people, thanks in large part to the tender guidance and nurturing of their mom. Keri has always shown a quiet strength, which has made her the rock of our family. Watch out for the shy ones—they always see things most clearly.

"No legacy is so rich as honesty."
—William Shakespeare (1564-1616)

TRUE SUCCESS

We are too quick to quantify success in terms of fortunes made and displayed through our possessions. Don't get me wrong—I love toys, sports cars, watches, etc., but those things do not define the true value of an individual. More important is what that person does to touch other people's lives. I am, like you, trying to find my way through this obstacle course called life.

I certainly have far more questions than answers. I do know the importance in my life of treating others with simple acts of kindness. A smile, a friendly hello, an unsolicited compliment or thank you…imagine how meaningful they can be to the person on the receiving end.

I go out of my way to do these things, not because that is how I want to be remembered, but because *that is how I choose to live.* How do you want to be remembered? What will be your legacy?

ACCEPTANCE

"Of course there is no formula for success
except perhaps an unconditional acceptance
of life and what it brings."
—Arthur Rubenstein (1886-1982)

THIS ONE IS TOUGH. Sometimes we get bad news—a business deal goes south, your car was hit, you lost your job, your home, who knows—it could be the most minor to the most major of events. Under my scenario, with just twenty-four hours to go, I don't have any time to waste. After all, I just have one day, and I certainly don't want to spend it ignoring the obvious—time is ticking.

It's easy—too easy—to fall into the trap of avoidance. It's the "see no evil, hear no evil" philosophy so many of us adopt. Rather than receive bad news and act on it, we ignore it, which ultimately makes matters much worse. It's the parking tickets left unpaid that result in your car being booted. It's the bills ignored that leave your credit in shambles. It's the small, unaddressed problems with your spouse that ignite major fights. It is impossible to solve any problem, if you don't first stop to identify and recognize that it exists. I suppose I allowed that to happen with my own finances and my career. I believed that everything would work out. I put faith in others to come through, when I should have taken steps myself to avoid the eventual bind I am now in.

My dear friends Steve and Josh both taught me the lessons of acceptance. So did Nicole. They didn't complain about the horrible news they'd each received from their doctors. They were disappointed and saddened, of course, at times even angry. We spent many hours talking about the randomness, the unfairness and the frustration of their illnesses. Still, each of them met their challenge head on. They *accepted* their diagnoses but did not give into them. Acceptance gave each of them the strength and composure needed to battle their illnesses. As a result, they each *lived* with dignity and *died* with dignity.

I have also finally accepted my parents for who they are, not for who I wanted them to be or how I wanted them to act, especially toward one another. There is no judgment and no blame to come from me. There is no need for either. I do, however, offer understanding. They are my parents, and I love each of them.

What about *your* problems? Deal with them and move forward. My wife's mom has a wonderful philosophy which she calls "putting your troubles in a box." She suggests you take all the negative feelings and energy around you and put them in an imaginary box. Then, place it high on a shelf, out of reach. This enables you to "let go" of those negative emotions, literally setting them aside, so you can move forward in a positive, constructive way. It sounds crazy at first, but I have to admit, I've tried it. That simple ritual has worked wonders for me many times. I have decided to incorporate it into my everyday life. Even on the last day of my life.

MIRACLES

"In order to be a realist you
must believe in miracles."
—Henry Christopher Bailey (1878-1961)

WHAT DO YOU SAY TO AN ELEVEN-YEAR-OLD BOY WHO
HOLDS OUT HIS HAND AND PLEADS WITH YOU TO TAKE THE
PAIN AWAY, WHILE YOU FEEL HELPLESS, TRYING IN VAIN TO
COMFORT HIM? This Thanksgiving, I heard one of the worst
sentences in the English language from the lips of my
beloved son, "It hurts so much, Daddy!" Matthew was
diagnosed with a little known nor understood syndrome:
RSD—Reflexive Sympathetic Dystrophy. RSD is
characterized by extreme nerve pain that can develop
following even a minor trauma or injury. In Matthew's case,
that injury was a sprained foot, which was, apparently,
improperly treated as a broken ankle. In a broad sense, RSD
is similar to a nerve being stuck in the "on" position,
constantly sending pain signals to the brain, even though
outwardly it looks as if nothing is wrong. The treatment is
multileveled, requiring physical, psychological and drug
therapies, essentially enabling the nervous system to "reboot"

much like a computer that is frozen in a program. Its complexity makes it so hard to properly identify.

Matthew was originally diagnosed as having a fracture in the growth plate of his left ankle, after accidentally being kicked while playing soccer at school. He was put in a cast for more than five weeks. For much of that time, Matthew continued to complain of severe pain in his foot. Still, his doctor assured us that Matthew was fine and to stay the course. Within a day of removing the cast, Matthew reinjured the ankle, and a soft, but restrictive, brace was substituted. Matthew's protests escalated to a point where he actually broke down in school following a fifth-grade assembly in which his class had performed a skit for the parents.

Matthew began crying and complaining of severe pain in his leg, despite wearing the splint that was prescribed by his doctor. Much to my chagrin, and in front of many of the other parents, his teacher employed a tough-love approach. Understandably, she believed that Matthew was using the outburst to seek attention and to avoid staying in school. The teacher shared with our son her displeasure over his pleas to go home and rest. After his mom spent an hour with him, allowing him to calm down, Matthew agreed to return to class. But the relief was short-lived. Within a day Matt was back at the doctor. That last visit was made all the more infuriating and confusing when that doctor, in the same medical group as the orthopedist who first placed Matthew in a cast, said flippantly, "He may never have broken his foot in the first place." Yet, he once again put Matthew's ankle in a cast.

Matthew's complaints persisted. In frustration, and out of growing concern, my wife sought out another pediatric orthopedist, who came highly recommended. That doctor removed the cast immediately and found Matthew's foot to be cold to the touch, and discolored, possibly indicating poor circulation. He told us that the lengthy immobilization of Matt's foot probably had a far worse impact than his original injury. This doctor felt that Matthew's complaints suggested a condition wholly apart from a sprain or a fracture. In fact, he also *did not believe the foot was ever fractured.* This physician immediately recognized the possibility that Matthew may in fact be suffering from RSD.

Our Thanksgiving holiday was a blur of medical visits, necessitated by Matthew's escalating protests of severe, almost debilitating pain. He was now unable to walk, and he spent most of his time in bed, crying or screaming. It was completely out of character for this mischievous prankster. He was unmoved to smile, even by the lure of a new video game. The pain and increasing anxiety made it impossible for him to focus on anything but his trauma.

On his new doctor's recommendation, Matthew received an MRI to his left foot. I spent forty-five minutes holding his hand while my baby lay motionless with his eyes closed in a machine that inspired in me an odd mixture of both confidence and trepidation. His body was too slight and his face too innocent to require a diagnostic tool of such solemnity and magnitude. Through each of the half-dozen cycles of the machine, it made a loud, odd clicking noise that required earplugs to dampen. During each respite, I spoke tenderly and reassuringly to Matthew. I told him stories that I hoped would soothe his fears and enable him to remain calm and still, so we could get a clear picture for the radiologist to examine.

Two days later, at his doctor's suggestion, we took him to the UCLA Emergency Room for another exam and some pain medication. The following day we went back to the orthopedist who suggested another MRI, this one to his lower spine. Finally, we took Matthew to be examined by a pediatric neurologist. All of the diagnoses pointed to the same frightening syndrome.

For several weeks, day and night, this normally outgoing, funny child with a beautiful face and bright smile was reduced to moaning and whimpering in pain, pleading with us to make it stop. Nerve medication was prescribed, increased and then changed. No dosage was sufficient to stop or even reduce his searing agony. Even Methadone proved useless against the burning, crushing pain Matthew described.

We were told it would take time. Those are difficult if not impossible words to process when you see your child suffering.

Keri and I could do little more than hold him while he cried. Caressing his body against our own, we lovingly stroked his hair and assured him that we knew his pain was real and that we knew that, eventually, it would go away. It is a powerless and humbling experience to look into the eyes of an innocent child, especially your own, who has always relied on you for protection, when you have nothing to offer but love, tenderness and empty promises.

I tried on many occasions to shield my face from him so he would not see me cry. I made several trips to the sink to splash my face with cold water to reduce the redness of my eyes. One night, Matthew caught me crying as I lay beside him, even though I did my best to turn away. He wiped a tear from my eyelash with a single, gentle swipe of his hand. In a meek but reassuring voice, he asked me not to cry as it made him even sadder, knowing that I was so unhappy.

"The most astonishing thing about miracles is that they happen."
—G.K. Chesterton (1874-1936)

Miracles can happen. I have witnessed one, and I remain humbled and grateful by the experience.

After days of consoling our son, taking him from one specialist to another, we finally embarked on a course of treatment overseen by one amazing and empathetic doctor, Lonnie Zeltzer, a specialist in psychiatry, anesthesiology and pediatrics who heads the UCLA Pediatric Pain Management Unit at the Mattel Children's Hospital. This woman was an expert in diagnosing and treating cases of pediatric RSD. Her unit is a destination of last resort for parents across the United States seeking definitive treatment for their children. Fortunately for us, that hospital was just a mile from our home.

When the doctor first examined our son, she appeared immune to his screams and protests. Despite his tears, her demeanor remained unchanged—calm and loving toward Matthew, listening attentively as he described the location and intensity of his pain. She gave us a list of specialists within her unit who would treat our son. Their areas of expertise embraced western and eastern approaches to medicine, from psychology to hypno-therapy, from acupuncture to physical therapy. The doctor told us in a gentle but matter of fact tone that our son's pain was both serious and severe, but that she had seen many cases that were far worse. Most importantly, she assured us that Matthew would get better in time.

The next month took its toll on our family, spiritually, mentally and physically. While it was hardest on Matthew, Keri and I spent so many nights lying awake, crying, worrying and studying up on this syndrome, which had overtaken our household. It didn't feel at all like Christmas was approaching, and it certainly didn't seem like a joyous time of year.

Matthew had already missed several weeks of school, and it was appearing less and less likely that even with the school break as a buffer that he would be able to return to his studies and his classmates after the first of the year. His pain level seemed impervious to both treatment and medication. His entire foot from just above the ankle down the sole was so sensitive that even a breeze or the slightest touch would send him into convulsions. As a result, he was unable to rest it under or even on top of the bedcovers.

I fashioned a foam cushion with makeshift cutouts to support his calf, allowing his foot to remain safely elevated above the bed. Even the thought of accidentally touching his foot now inspired terror in our boy. When he would inadvertently brush his foot against anything, as he often would throughout the day or night, he would immediately respond with a deafening scream, followed by tears and uncontrollable shaking. It was simply the worst thing I had ever witnessed as a parent.

Then, suddenly, after more than a month, and after being told by the specialists to expect weeks if not longer of the same, I was sitting alongside Matthew as he struggled to maintain focus while playing a video game. He turned to me and said, quite calmly, "I think the bottom of my foot doesn't hurt any more."

"What?" I wasn't really sure what I had just heard.

"I think it's fine," he said. Before I could fully process what he was saying, he reached over and stroked the bottom of his foot with his right hand. *There was no pain!* Then, he exclaimed that the sides of his left foot and the front of his shin also felt normal. He touched those areas as well with the same result— *no pain at all*. Without hesitating, he stood, for the first time in a month and tried to walk. He began tentatively, but with each step his confidence swelled. My son was walking!

Matthew was not cured—the top of his foot and toes still tortured him. The pain in those areas remained unchanged and quite intense. Still, in a single moment, he was no longer a patient without hope. He was again an eleven-year-old boy who not only believed but also now *knew* that he would be cured. He began to laugh, and I soon joined him as I yelled out to my wife to run into his room. Together, we watched as our son took his first steps in weeks. It may sound like the most ordinary of mornings, but for us it was nothing short of a miracle.

Within two days, my son surprised me again. The condition had rendered Matthew's left foot far too sensitive to wear even a sock, and yet, there he was, wearing the new pair of tennis shoes his sister had given him as an early Christmas present. He looked different—calm, rested and clean. He told me that he took his first shower in a month. Water splashing his foot had previously stung like bullets, so for weeks he draped his left foot over the tub while taking a bath. I talk for a living, and yet, there I was, speechless.

Matthew proudly announced that all the pain was gone. He felt the area of pain literally shrink with the passing of each hour since he began walking again, and now he was completely normal. He performed a brief jog while smiling broadly just to prove his point. I felt a wave of euphoria wash over me, and I hugged Matthew so tightly I was afraid I might crush him. I don't know exactly how or why he was better, but I decided not to question it any further. If I ever had a reason not to believe in miracles, those doubts were erased right then and there. Our prayers had been heard, and they had been answered.

The amazing thing about miracles is that they can occur at any time, when you least expect them. Think about that last day and consider what miracles can happen, even then. I could never have imagined nor dreamed that the prayers for my son could be heard let alone answered as quickly and completely as they were—I guess that's what makes it a miracle after all. The important thing about miracles isn't that they happen. It's the belief that they **can** happen.

REDEMPTION

"The salvation of man is through love and in love."
—Viktor Frankl (1905-1997)

HERE ARE JUST THREE DEFINITIONS OF REDEMPTION:

1. Rescue
2. Deliverance from sin, salvation
3. Atonement for guilt

I suspect that when it comes to redemption, you know it when you see it—or more accurately, when you *feel* it. It is closely tied to spiritualism and religion. The sense of deliverance and salvation are both acknowledgments of a greater good or higher power. Scholars have argued and written about the concepts for centuries, and I certainly would not presume to close the topic with a few paragraphs. But that's not the point. Rather, I am trying to allow you to open a dialogue with yourself about this concept that is, after all, most personal. No one else can lead you to redemption. It takes faith—a belief in something you cannot see or prove, but that you trust is there.

The wonderful thing about redemption is that it's never too late to seek it and to find it. It is at the end of the list for a reason — it is most difficult to achieve. Some people never do. Unlike adventure, which is a *spirit* from the *inside out*, redemption is *spiritual* and comes from the *outside in*. It involves the asking of forgiveness.

A wonderful thing happened to me on this journey of self-discovery. I found redemption. I have finally freed myself from the shackles of childhood guilt. I have discovered salvation through how I have chosen to live my own life. My own children joined in rescuing me. I am finally able to breathe freely. No more waiting in anticipation, anxious about what might happen. I am an adult. I have chosen my path, and I am not only comfortable with my decision, I am at peace with my decision.

> **"Maybe you have to know darkness**
> **before you can appreciate the light."**
> —Madeleine L'Engle (1918-2007)

FINDING MYSELF

It was, in fact, that darkness which compelled me to first recognize the many blessings in my life. *My redemption came in an instant.*

It happened on the morning of April 16, 2008, when I was driving on that lonely stretch of road in Malibu Canyon, imagining myself deliberately steering my car over the edge of the cliff. My detailed suicidal fantasy literally scared me straight. It caused me to shift my focus to those closest to me whom I would be leaving behind. At that moment, even though they weren't even with me at the time, Keri and our children literally saved my life.

In many ways, my son was actually my savior. From the time he could crawl, the word "dad" was synonymous with pal, hero and confidant. In just two years, he will be the age I was when my own identity was abruptly changed through my adoption. I had to give him something I never had—continuity and unconditional love from a father to a son. With all my children, when they say, "I love you daddy," my answer is always the same: "I love you more." Then we each have our mock argument over who loves each other the most. What a wonderful topic to dispute. What a glorious way to live. How could I voluntarily say goodbye to that? I couldn't. I wouldn't.

But the road I traveled to reach that discovery was actually much longer than that brief stretch of secluded Malibu asphalt. For years, my journey had a single question at its core: "Who am I?"

In my early childhood, my identity appeared to be up for grabs. My last name and initials had been changed so many times before my thirteenth birthday that it became a running gag among my friends. Then, my adoption stripped me of my original identity as James William Ercolani Jr. and officially reintroduced me to the world as James William Moret. In fact, as far as my birth certificate showed, I had never even had a different name.

At eighteen, my closest childhood friend, Steve, was taken from me. At twenty-five, my already tenuous relationship with my biological father was suspended for a few years following the flap over my wedding ceremony. It marked my third major break with my father: his divorce from my mom, my adoption and then my wedding. At thirty-eight, my best friend, Josh, passed away, taking with him more memories unique to the two of us.

Growing up, I was always the perfect child. I have long recognized my overwhelming desire and need to be liked. I eventually chose a high-profile job in broadcasting that, almost by definition, required being liked by the public. *There are no accidents.*

In my mid-forties, my *professional* identity felt in jeopardy for a few years after I left CNN. It had been my safe haven, my home for nearly a decade. One thing I learned about being a news anchor or television host: when your show is cancelled, you begin to lose sight of who you are. I began to joke with my wife that I should set up a camera and desk in our living room, so I could interview people as they came to our door. I simply didn't know what to do. It felt like an important part of me was missing, if not gone.

Looking back at my life, as one is apt to do when thinking about ending theirs, I now recognize and embrace all the valuable lessons of gratitude, friendship and love, sacrifice and commitment, forgiveness and apology, understanding and compassion, tenacity, music and laughter, adventure and passion, possessions, surprise and wonder, purpose and legacy, acceptance, redemption and hope.

WHO AM I?

I am the product of all those experiences. *I am a husband, a father, a son, a brother, an uncle, a friend, a musician, a lawyer and a broadcaster.*

If I have learned nothing else, it is to keep on going, no matter what. Giving up is not an option. It shows a disregard and lack of respect to those people closest to me: those who taught me, love me and still want and need me around. To them, I am *not* worth more dead than alive, no matter how big the insurance policy.

Ultimately, of course, rather than *ending* my life, I chose to truly *live* my life. At the beginning of this book, I shared some of my anguish that led me down that frightening path. Am I still dealing with many of those same challenges? Of course I am. Life is *never* problem-free. Despite the challenges I face I am determined never again to lose my sense of self.

What is now different is my *perspective* on the importance of the issues facing me throughout my life and my *decision* to make sure they never again overshadow the *blessings* in my life. I cannot control all the curveballs that life throws me. None of us can. But I can measure my reaction to those surprises. *Ironically, if I had not hit my emotional rock bottom, I would never have made it this far along my journey of enlightenment.*

I am sure that there are plenty of struggles and frustrations that lie ahead for me. But I have a renewed clarity now about what is really important to me. *Living* is at the top of the list.

TWENTY-FOUR HOUR CHECKLIST

**"The great end of life
is not knowledge, but action."**
—Thomas Fuller (1608-1661)

TAKE THE TIME AND MAKE YOUR OWN CHECKLIST FOR
THE LAST DAY OF *YOUR* LIFE.

Where would you like to go?

What would you hope to see?

Would you offer anyone an apology or seek
forgiveness?

To whom would you show gratitude, compassion,
and understanding?

Which friends and loved ones would you gather with
to share the joy of laughter?

What music would serve as the soundtrack to your
final day?

What would you choose as your last true adventure?

What was your greatest passion?

What surprise will you cherish most?
What was your life's purpose and legacy?
What is your Perfect Day?

"Don't let it get away
It's a beautiful day."
—U2

In order to determine what I would want to do on the last day of my life, I think immediately of those things that would represent my *perfect* day—a day involving those events, activities and people that make life most meaningful to me.

REVISITING THE LAST DAY OF MY LIFE

"As soon as you trust yourself,
you will know how to live."
—Johann Wolfgang von Goethe (1749-1832)

MY TOUGHEST INTERVIEW

As I suspected at the outset of this journey, asking myself the questions posed the most difficult endeavor, not of my career but of my life. The challenge, of course, came in answering those questions. The most serious of them all was, "Do I want to live?" I now answer with a definitive *yes*. I tried to be honest. I have discovered that fooling oneself can only be accomplished for so long before it is revealed as a lie. I also recognize that the truth I uncovered is more accurately *"my truth,"* not necessarily *"the truth"* in an absolute sense. When dealing with feelings and emotions, I am not sure that an absolute truth really exists anyway.

I have learned that every life is precious and limited. We know there is a beginning and there is an end. We do not know *when* that end will come. I have seen too many people close to me fight and cling to life to ever again entertain the thought of deliberately ending my own. We are never told in advance how long we have to pursue our dreams. So I move forward now, armed with a new perspective, renewed faith and optimism. Of course, we must all plan for the future, but we can still choose to be engaged in the present, living in the moment for each and every moment. I am now striving to be truly present and engaged. Wonder and joy are experienced throughout the *journey;* they are not only discovered at the *destination.*

Imagine now that *you* had only one day left to live. How would you choose to spend it?

Will you be alone in a room, sulking and waiting for the inevitable, or will you use that time to reach out to others in friendship, love and compassion?

Will you share the joys of music and laughter?

Would you take the time to apologize and to forgive?

How much of your precious day focuses on what makes you grateful, on the sacrifices and commitments you have made?

Are you approaching the experience with tenacity and purpose?

Will you revel in the surprises and wonders that even one day can offer?

Would you face the time with hope and allow acceptance and redemption into your heart?

Would you seek to experience your perfect day?

HELLO, GOODBYE

Several years ago, while at the services for my friend, Larry, I was struck by the randomness and suddenness of his death. He never had one last chance to say goodbye to the people who meant the most to him. He had not only lived life, he embraced it. While he said so much through his actions, what might he have said to all of us if he had only had the chance?

I decided at that moment to take the unorthodox approach of preparing my final farewell in advance. I wrote a letter and placed it in a safe, with instructions that it was to be read aloud after the last day of my life.

Some people say it's not important how long one lives but rather HOW one lives. I lived pretty damn well.

I am blessed with a loving family. I married the sweetest, most beautiful girl I'd ever seen, who blossomed into an even more breathtaking woman with a grace and a quiet strength and enduring love which continued to amaze me. I was fortunate to marry her not once, but again twenty years later.

We are blessed with three amazing children: Amanda—my twin as she liked to call herself—a talented, self-assured and serious student of film and of life; Carly, the carefree beauty and carbon copy of Keri, who could disarm with a glance; and Matthew, my "mini-me" who makes us all laugh and wonder how could we have ever lived without him.

My mom—for several years it was her and me against the world—me a toddler and she a child, growing up together against the odds and winning. Her grit and unwavering determination made much of my life possible. We were both so lucky that she met Gery. I have called him dad since I was six, and he earned that title every single day and wore it proudly all my life. I remain proud to have him call me son.

My father—we spent so much of our lives sparring over the past—mistakes, would haves, should haves, could haves, and every once in a while we both came to our senses and realized that the present was all we could really count on, so let's not waste it. He loved me the best he could, and it was enough for me. I am glad he and my mom were together long enough for me to be here and enjoy the ride.

Keri's parents Horty and Artie—a cross between Ozzie and Harriet and Archie and Edith—were always as loving and devoted to me as if I were their own son. What an honor—to have another set of parents.

My sweet sister, Holly—Hollard I liked to call her— who never stopped believing in me, was a joy as a baby and a delight as an adult, for me, and especially for my kids.

My brothers, Christian and Anthony, whom I never saw nearly enough but loved very much.

If a man's wealth is defined by his friends, then I was truly rich. I never grew tired of playing, laughing, joking and hanging out with them. Some of you I saw less often than I would have liked, but so many of you showed me the meaning of friendship when it was most difficult to do so. When I was in need, you were there to give me confidence and courage. Hopefully, I repaid you in kind. I never lost the feeling of being a kid.

I did just about everything I ever dreamed of doing. I piloted an airplane (several in fact). I took a helicopter lesson. I drove an Indy car, a midget racer and a Shelby Cobra around the Las Vegas Motor Speedway. I trained at Willow Springs and competed in the Long Beach Grand Prix Pro Celebrity Race (I came in sixth out of fourteen, and I spun out in the third lap). I bought a Harley-Davidson and trained for and got my motorcycle license. I drove most of my adult life in a convertible, because I was never content simply looking ahead, and I was always in a sports car, because life shouldn't be bound by speed limits.

I got to see so much of the world firsthand—from Paris, my favorite city where I followed Keri when we were in college and where we returned more than a dozen years later—together, to the Pyramids in Egypt, to climbing the Harbor Bridge in Sydney, Australia, to spending a week in Dracula's Castle in Transylvania. Most of you thought I was crazy to go but I'm glad I did.

I played my alter ego, "Conrad Birdie" in my high school play and never gave up on the idea that being a rock star sounded pretty good to me. I took guitar lessons well into my forties. I finally built my own studio before I turned forty-five, and after three decades of playing the same Allman Brothers, James Taylor and Eagles songs over and over, I finally became a decent musician.

After being a lawyer and following a mercifully brief stint as a garment manufacturer (the one year I wish I could forget) I found the perfect job for me—one where I got PAID to TALK. For the better part of a decade I got to interview some of my musical heroes including Eric Clapton, B.B. King, Larry Carlton and Carlos Santana. I got to hang out with the Eagles and count Elton John, Davey Johnstone and

Robben Ford among my friends. I never got to host the Today
Show *or* Good Morning America, *but filling in for Larry King
wasn't too shabby. I did what I loved and loved what I did.*

*I consider myself one of the luckiest people I know,
blessed with so much and mindful of how temporary this
all really is.*

*They say "you can't take it with you," so instead, I
leave part of myself with each of you to do with as you wish.
I hope you enjoyed our time together as much as I did.*

I had actually forgotten about that letter until Keri
discovered it in our safe when looking for our passports. She
found it while I was writing this final chapter! *Again, I believe
this was not an accident.*

At the time I wrote it, Keri thought it was morbid,
but I believed then, and I am now convinced, that it was
actually empowering. It may have been intended as a
farewell, but its focus was really on *life* not *death*. Writing it
forced me to examine the *positive*, not the *negative* in my
life. *My real mistake was keeping it out of sight and out of
my mind once it was written.* Reading it again for the first
time in years reminded me why I loved my life and needed
to keep living as long as possible. *Looking back gave me every
reason to look forward.* What a valuable exercise and an
indispensable lesson.

DAILY MIRROR THERAPY

"And since you know you cannot see yourself,
so well as by reflection, I, your glass,
will modestly discover to yourself,
that of yourself which you yet know not of."
—William Shakespeare (1564-1616)

Every morning, before setting off for the next 24 hours, I find it a good time to reflect on the previous day. If those hours had been my last, was it time well spent? Were those minutes I traded worth the results? Did I spend them doing something positive and constructive or was I stuck in idle or, worse still, was I locked in reverse?

How were *your* last twenty-four hours spent? Was the last day of your life a good day? How could you have made it better, or more meaningful and productive? There are no second chances here. You cannot go *back*, but you can move *forward* with a difference.

Incorporate this routine into your daily life. Look in the mirror every morning and use it as an opportunity to look back on your previous day. If you are truly honest with yourself, it will give you all the momentum you need to move forward with purpose.

BRINGING MOTION TO EMOTION

"Cherish your own emotions
and never undervalue them."
—Robert Henri (1865-1929)

What if your *next* twenty-four hours were your *best* twenty-four hours? Imagine it being the first time you told someone how much you loved him or her or finally let go of the anger or resentment you had harbored for so long that it had literally eaten away at your spirit. Wouldn't you hope to do something meaningful if you know those next hours were your final hours? Think how motivated you would be to make sure your last day would be a memorable one. If you embrace each new day with that philosophy, then just think how meaningful each moment could be. Why *hope* things can happen when you can *make* them happen? Take action. Choose your direction and then go. Don't just hold onto feelings. Express them. Bring **motion to your emotion** and imagine living each day as if it were your last day. You will end up cherishing each and every day thereafter as the gift that it can be.

RESETTING MY 24-HOUR CLOCK

"I must govern the clock, not be governed by it."
—Golda Meir (1898-1978)

THE GOOD NEWS, OF COURSE, IS THAT THIS IS *NOT* MY LAST DAY. But each morning, I now take a moment and *mentally reset* my "twenty-four hour clock." I imagine that I have only one day left. How will I spend it? It is a fictional ritual with very real results. It literally shapes the day before me and puts it in a context, which yields tangible results.

I have decided to embrace each day *as if it was my last* and focus exclusively on the positive influences and people around me. In that way, I believe that the *rest* of my life will be immeasurably more rewarding, more joyous and more meaningful. Imagine that **it took me contemplating my own death to teach me how to truly live.** Sometimes, the most obvious lessons are the most difficult to learn.

I have not yet reached my destination. I am committed to continuing on this journey of my life no matter what happens along the way.

I have come to view *time* as my *friend*.

I will cherish it, guard it, use it and make the most of it. I plan to live the *rest of my life* as if this were the *last day of my life*.

ACKNOWLEDGMENTS

Writing is a long, lonely process, but this book would not have been possible without the support, encouragement and blind faith placed in me by so many people.

To my friends, Tony Coghlan, Nicole Ullerich, and Ami Desai, who read my first notes when this book was just an idea, thank you for encouraging me to continue. My brother, Christian, a gifted writer, spent hours with me on the phone, guiding me through our often painful pasts in an effort to free me to put my thoughts to paper. When I told him how difficult this was, he said. "That's why writers drink."

When I wondered if anyone would represent me, my friend David Lonner, a theatrical agent, read it and believed in it enough to pass it on to his colleague Mel Berger in New York. I still remember my first phone conversation with Mel where he admitted, "Here I am reading something from someone I don't know, telling me about other people I don't know, and I can't put it down." Mel has been my advocate, my champion and my agent ever since, and we never met face to face before my book was completed.

Michael Viner first expressed his interest when my book was still in an early stage. A dear mutual friend, Bonnie Tiegel, sent my manuscript to him telling him he had to read it. Months later, when we ran into each other at Nate 'n Al's deli, he said, "I still want to publish your book." Michael's belief and vision brought my dream to reality. Michael's last words to me were, "I'm proud of you." Michael, it is you to whom I am indebted and shall always be grateful. I miss you already.

I was so fortunate to find in Dan Smetanka an editor with purpose, passion and a real understanding of what I hoped to accomplish with this book. Dan's guidance made me a better writer. Writing may be hard, but I loved editing.

Even after writing and editing there was so much work to be done. Donna Dees was my guardian angel, cheering and steering me in the right direction with endless enthusiasm. Donna is an amazing publicist and a true friend.

Finally, I want to thank all the people who are featured in this book, because your lives have shaped mine, and in the process you have made me realize the importance and blessings in living.